CELEBRATION OF HAND-HOOKED RUGS XXV
2015 Edition

Editor
Debra Smith

Coordinator
Sandy Oravec

Designer
CW Design Solutions, Inc.

Advertising Coordinator
Gail Weaverling

Customer Service
Publisher's Service Associates
U.S. (877) 297-0965
Canada (866) 375-8626

Operations Manager
Anne Lodge

Publisher
Judith Schnell

Rug photographs provided by the artists unless otherwise noted.

Rug Hooking magazine is published five times a year in Jan./Feb., March/April/May, June/July/Aug., Sept./Oct., and Nov./Dec. by Stackpole, Inc., 5067 Ritter Road, Mechanicsburg, PA 17055. *Celebration of Hand-Hooked Rugs* is published annually. Contents Copyright© 2015. All rights reserved. Reproduction in whole or part without the written consent of the publisher is prohibited. Canadian GST #R137954772.

A Publication of

R·U·G HOOKING

5067 Ritter Road
Mechanicsburg, PA 17055
(717) 796-0411
www.rughookingmagazine.com
rughook@stackpolebooks.com

ISBN-978-0-8117-1636-9

Printed in U.S.A.

WELCOME TO CELE

Happy Anniversary!

Twenty five years . . . can you believe it? It has been a quarter of a century since the very first *Celebration of Hand-Hooked Rugs* was published in 1991. Those were the days of Teenage Mutant Ninja Turtles, *Beauty and the Beast* in the theatre, *Cheers* on television, Natalie Cole's haunting "Unforgettable" on the radio, and the very first Starbucks coffee shop. My, how far we have come!

Celebration I featured 24 hooked rugs in a 58-page book, an intriguing time capsule of rug hooking from the early 1990s. As we began to work on this 25th Anniversary edition, we realized that many of those featured artists and honorable mention creators are still hooking 25 years later. In a wonderful full-circle sort of way, Peggy Hannum, whose *Swirls* you see on the cover of this book, was one of those finalists 25 years ago. Peggy was quoted on the jacket cover: "Hooking is my relaxation, my therapy . . . It satisfies my addiction for the beautiful, the subtle, the colorful, and the tactile." I know that what she said then is as true today as it was in 1991.

Has rug hooking changed over the last quarter of a century? Well, yes and no. The same high quality work, phenomenal color planning, and creative designs grace the pages of that very first *Celebration* and the pages of the book you are holding in your hands. Today's finalists are just as daring and original as the hookers of 1991. And while you may find a few more bits and bobs of untraditional fibers and embellishments in today's rugs, you will surely notice the same themes: landscapes, creatures, flora and fauna, people, and stories. The colors might be a bit brighter and more dramatic, there are fewer 8-value roses, and the rugs may be somewhat less formal in design, but we readily see that rug hooking today is alive and well and thriving.

After all, we still hook rugs for the same reasons today. We seek to capture in fiber what is important in our lives; we design rugs and pull loops to celebrate those moments and ideas, to make them permanent in our chosen medium of linen and wool. And in doing so, we satisfy our need to create, design, and memorialize . . . even as we create hooked-rug heirlooms for future generations.

I wonder what the next 25 years will bring. What will be on the cover of *Celebration L* (50)? Maybe it will be a rug hooked by one of the talented rug hookers in this very book.

Thank you to all the rug hookers who have participated and supported *Celebration* over the last quarter of a century. We are in awe of your artistry and creativity, your generosity and enthusiasm, and we celebrate your accomplishments and the beauty you bring to the world through your fabulous pieces.

It has been our great honor to sponsor this annual event for 25 years, and we look forward to (at least) 25 more!

Readers' Choice
Remember to vote for your favorite hooked rugs to be a part of the Readers' Choice decision. Use the enclosed ballot and return it to us by **December 31, 2015.**

On the Cover: Swirl, *hooked by Peggy Hannum, 2014. For more information about this fabulous Heirloom rug, see page 60.*

Table of Contents

RUGS BASED ON ADAPTATIONS

RUGS BASED ON PRIMITIVE DESIGNS

HONORABLE MENTIONS

Meet the Judges

Each year a new panel of judges takes on the daunting task of evaluating *Celebration* entries. Imagine the enormity of the task: each entry comes with 4 separate photos, so in a field of 200 entries the judges will review and evaluate a total of 800 photographs. With our current system of online judging, the process is more judge-friendly than in the days when judges traveled here to view the entries, one slide at a time. But consider the task that they face: even sitting in their own homes in a favorite chair with a cup of coffee nearby, it is an enormous commitment of time and energy. Hours and hours of concentration, deliberation, and careful consideration; the judges essentially commit one week in early January to *Celebration* judging. All for the love of rug hooking. It is their expertise and wide-ranging experience that makes *Celebration* work so well; they are the foundation of the whole enterprise.

And so we extend our heartfelt thanks to these four judges and to all the judges who have gone before them. And, please . . . if you have an opportunity, be sure to thank a judge. Their contributions cannot be overstated.

Jen Lavoie

Jen has been hooking for almost 30 years. Her work is pictorial, realistic, and nature-themed. She uses all cut sizes and appreciates all styles of expression. Her rugs have been featured in many articles and books. She has been 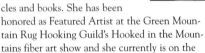 honored as Featured Artist at the Green Mountain Rug Hooking Guild's Hooked in the Mountains fiber art show and she currently is on the board and is Show Chair for Hooked in the Mountains. Rug hooking as an art form is her passion as well as her sanctuary. She is passionate about learning, finding new ways to express herself through fiber, and sharing her knowledge as a teacher.

Diane Phillips

For the last 19 years, Diane has been passionate about creating hand-hooked art. These days she is playing with unusual uses of color: "A touch of the surreal or unexpected holds our attention in paintings and other media. I 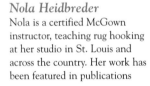 believe rugs deserve this spark of magic also." She is also attracted to unusual groupings, mixing motifs of living things with organic shapes, and experimental color palettes. She has taught in the U.S. (including Maui), Canada, and Great Britain, and has been a "Featured Artist" for the Green Mountain Rug Hooking Guild and Sauder Village. She directed the Green Mountain Hooked in the Mountains Workshops for eight years. She retired to explore other art forms, now experimenting with wearables, jewelry, and wet felting—all combined with touches of rug hooking.

Nola Heidbreder

Nola is a certified McGown instructor, teaching rug hooking at her studio in St. Louis and across the country. Her work has been featured in publications such as *Mary Engelbreit's Home Companion Magazine*, *Rug Hooking* magazine, *The Healthy Planet* newspaper, the *ATHA* newsletter, *Hooked on Rugs*, *Creative Hooker*, *Hooked on Wool*, *Hooked Rugs Today*, and *Contemporary Hooked Rugs*. Selected pieces been included in *The "Art" of Playing Cards* traveling rug hooking exhibit and catalog, and were exhibited twice in the Coalition for the Environment show. Nola hooked all 44 U.S. presidents in the 2013 Special Exhibit of Hooked and Knitted Presidents. The collection received the 2013 Sauder "Collection" Award. Together with her sister, Linda Pietz, she wrote and published the book *Hooking the Presidents* to accompany the exhibit. In 2014, Nola and Linda co-authored *Knitting Rugs* (Stackpole Books, 2014). Their book *Crocheting Rugs* will be published in late 2015 by Stackpole Books.

Karen Kahle

Karen, who holds a bachelor's degree in art, is a fiber artist in Eugene, Oregon. Her work can be seen in past issues of *Celebration* and *Rug Hooking* magazine. For the past 14 years, she has hooked and designed rugs for her business, Primitive Spir-  it, which specializes in designs in the primitive style of rug hooking: vintage, stylized, with soft, time-worn colors. She also travels to teach classes and workshops on color. She has published dye books that feature her antique colors, as well as *The Marbleized Wool Book*, about creating colorful wool without using dyes.

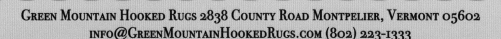

Basket Weave

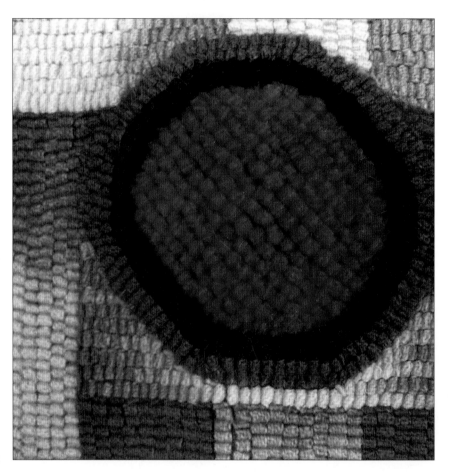

Most of the 25 rugs Debbie Mann has hooked since 1999 are original designs, and about half of those "are inspired by dyed wool that I buy simply because it caught my eye." And that's kind of the story behind this rug.

"I was inspired by a dye sampler that Jane Olson had at a Cambria Pines Retreat. I was enthralled by the three-dimensional illusion it created by the way the wool was dyed and hooked."

Jane passed away before the retreat, but her granddaughter, Brigitta Phy, was there.

Debbie showed her a picture she had taken of the sampler and asked Brigitta if she could replicate the colors. "Brigitta drew the design based on my description, but because of the nature of the dye on the wool, I had to modify my design."

Then, "while I was hooking part of the rug one night, I suddenly wanted a splash of bright red on it. I don't know why this popped into my head, but I just went with it. This red spot appears to hover on top of the weave."

The rug took more than a year to finish, and the design had its particular challenges:

"Because of how the wool was dyed, dark to light to dark, I had to draw the weave design as I completed each segment. The wool strips were finite. I could not add any more wool to each line; the strip was the total length of the segment. The original design did not fit the length of the dyed strips, so I had to hook over and past the original design lines, and draw new lines as I hooked."

The rug was finished by wrapping the burlap ends over twine, whip stitching, and hand sewing binding tape.

Debbie started rug hooking after reading an article in *Martha Stewart Living* magazine. She bought a hook at a wool store, wool clothing at a thrift shop, drew a simple design on burlap, and plunged in. Jane Olson gave her her first formal instruction at a rug hooking guild in San Luis Obispo, California.

Jane "was an inspiration" to Debbie. "I miss her wit and her creativity. I was very lucky to have met her. Her designs

DEBBIE MANN
SANTA MARIA, CALIFORNIA

Debbie works in civil service and hooks as an enjoyable artistic outlet. She bought her first rug pattern, Jane Olson's Exotica, *at the same meeting where she took her first lesson because "I thought it so beautiful. I did not have the confidence to start that rug until 2005. I entered Exotica in the Santa Barbara County Fair and won Best of Show." This is her work's first appearance in* Celebration.

*Basket Weave, 25" x 23^1/$_2$", #4- and 5-cut wool on burlap.
Designed and hooked by Debbie Mann, Santa Maria, California, 2014.*

and use of color are wonderful, and she (with her sister Norma) was a very funny and enjoyable person and teacher!"

Lessons learned from this rug: "I want to make more 3D basket-weave rugs in different colors. Brigitta has already dyed some burgundy wool for me; I just drew up a new design."

In the Judges' Eyes

- *Very original, outstanding trompe l'oeil; obvious hooking skill; weaving looks spot-on; had to be so difficult to hook!*

Beltie

Karen Poetzinger was drawn to create this rug because of the story behind it.

"I snapped the photo that inspired this piece in the spring. This little guy and his mama were in a small corner area of the pasture where their keepers would feed them. This little guy had had his fill and was heading back out to the field for a romp when he suddenly realized he did not have his mama with him. He looked back over his shoulder to find her and his expression said, 'Hey mom, let's go!' I just loved his expression and body position."

Karen's rug-hooking journey began in 1979 while home on fall break from college. Her mother had taken up rug hooking and "it intrigued me. I had always loved doing hands-on arts and crafts. I had done sewing, quilting, and painting as well as other crafty things. I sat down at my mother's frame and just went at it. That Christmas my mother gifted me with a pattern, wool, stripper, and frame. My first rug was Pearl McGown's *Paisley*."

Karen used mainly 8-value swatches and "bits of this and that" for Beltie himself. "The fence and ground are overdyes and spots"—all new wool. Her favorite elements of the rug are the calf's expression and body position.

Beltie took a few months to hook and now resides in Karen's studio, "where he makes me smile every time I look at him." This piece won best original piece at the Merrie Mountain Rug Hookers annual hook-in in the fall of 2014.

Karen finished the rug by first lacing it to foam board. She then had a custom suede mat and frame made "and sandwiched it all together."

Challenges with this piece included "getting the expression and depth. Making sure I had enough contrast to get the needed depth and perspective in the calf. As with every piece I do, I always find that your darks have to be darker than you initially expect. And that your lights have to be lighter. Contrast is what makes a piece pop."

In the Judges' Eyes

- *Compelling story, with nice shading and diagonal composition; subtle colors and unusual positioning of the subject are very effective; lovely piece.*

Beltie, 28" x 28", #4-cut wool on linen. Designed and hooked by Karen Poetzinger, Pittsboro, North Carolina, 2013.

KAREN POETZINGER
PITTSBORO, NORTH CAROLINA

Karen has been a McGown Certified Instructor since 1998 and served as treasurer for Southeastern Workshop. She is a juried member of the Piedmont Craftsmen Guild in Winston-Salem, North Carolina, as well as the Carolina Designer Craftsmen Guild in Raleigh. Her work has won awards in local art competitions, and her rug Madrigal received an Honorable Mention in Celebration III. She is a member of her local chapter of ATHA, the Piedmont Rug Hookers, where she has held the positions of president and treasurer. She teaches classes in her home studio and at workshops.

Bucknam Benson's House at Seal Cove

line without having to use a finer cut. I also like the complimentary color combinations, purple beside gold and pink beside green. I also like the lattice work under the porch, which I hooked with a black and white houndstooth check. I used little bits of woolen yarn in the window reflections. I used tweeds in the window reflections and for the roof. I like how the light hits on one side of the house and how it makes an angled patch of light on the ell of the house." Most challenging? The sky. "I was in suspense the whole time. 'Was I going to have enough wool to hook the sky?' that was the question."

A graduate of the Ontario College of Art and Design and a rug hooking teacher with the Ontario Hooking Craft Guild, Trish likes hooking pictorial rugs, "especially landscapes with buildings. I am interested in the sky, the weather, the light, and the shadows. I think of my style as impressionistic. I frequently include text."

Trish has hooked 45 rugs since she began in 1990. Lessons from this one? "I learned that I should have dyed a wider piece for the sky. I had to move some of the sky around and re-hook it."

Bucknam Benson's House was shown at The Pumphouse Gallery in Niagara on the Lake, Todmorden Mills, in Toronto, and the Ontario Hooking Craft Guild Annual in London, Ontario.

"Most of my rugs are story rugs. My great-great-grandfather, Seward Bucknam Benson (1838 – 1899) lived in this house at Seal Cove, on Grand Manan Island in New Brunswick. Bucknam's daughter, my great-grandmother Wealtha Irene Benson, wrote on a postcard, 'This is our home on Grand Manan where I was born and brought up.'" This work is part of a series of rugs depicting places that are significant in Johnson's family history.

Trish dip dyed the sky. "The rest of the wool I had in my stash. The whitewashed cedar shingle house is a mixture of leftover partial swatches and dip dyes." She hooked some of the field with some recycled, as-is tweeds.

"The field is my favorite part of the rug because it was the least challenge to hook. It hooked easily and was fun to hook. It has a looser, less-perfectionistic style. I used a lot of tweeds in the field, which had the effect of giving me a finer

---

TRISH JOHNSON
TORONTO, ONTARIO, CANADA

This is the ninth work by Trish Johnson that has appeared in Celebration. *She has never sold a rug, but "I exhibit my rugs whenever I can." She is "a wife, mother, grandmother, photographer, rug hooker, and quilter," and was named Canadian Rug Hooking Artist of the Year by The Hooked Rug Museum of North America in 2014.*

She is a member of The Georgetown Rug Hooking Guild, The Upper Toronto Rug Hooking Guild, and The Teachers' Branch of The Ontario Hooking Craft Guild.

Bucknam Benson's House at Seal Cove, 31" x 26 1/4", #4- and 6-cut wool and woolen yarn on linen. Designed and hooked by Trish Johnson, Toronto, Ontario, Canada, 2014. NORTHERN ARTISTS

In the Judges' Eyes

- *Great perspective keeps the viewer intrigued; beautiful portrayal of this house from a unique and difficult angle; wonderful contrast with the sky, house, and foreground; closer inspection reveals subtle color detail.*

Gartenstraße (Garden Street)

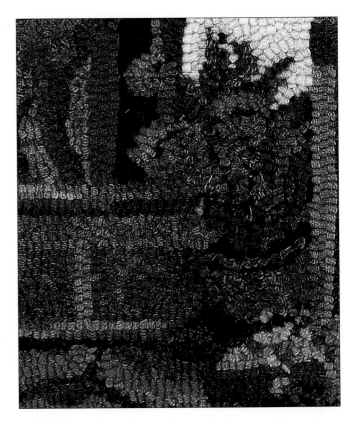

"My daughter Stephanie and her husband, Jason, sponsored an exchange student in 2007-2008. We were in Germany in 2010 to visit Anna, meet her family, and explore the country." This is the home of Anna's mother, Eva, in Ottenhofen, Germany, a village outside of Munich. "Eva was serving us dessert and coffee on a table in a sunken patio when I took this shot. I knew as soon as I saw this photograph that I would eventually hook it."

Linda Powell started this rug in July 2014 when two local guilds hosted a mini-worshop with Donna Hrkman. The piece was completed in November. "A special thank you to Donna for starting me on the right foot by suggesting a few subtle design changes."

The perspective was the most challenging part of the rug. Owing to the perspective from which the original photograph was taken, "a few items looked distorted when hooked exactly like the photo. One was the right arm of the bench. Because my view was 'straight on' with the left arm, you were able to see the complete inside edge of the right arm. But when I hooked it that way, it looked like the arm was broken. So I re-hooked it, angling it less, then added more of the flowers and leaf foliage. Trying to get the stones in the stone walkway to look flat and receding also proved difficult. I continued to switch out different shades of wool, in addition to altering the shapes slightly, until they looked more pleasing."

Her favorite parts are the stone steps and the open door. "They take me back to one of the most memorable places I have ever been. I don't think I stopped smiling (inside and out) the entire time I was hooking this project."

Which is maybe why the rug's lesson was "to hook what makes me smile and to continue to challenge myself."

Linda completed the piece with a custom frame. She mounted and laced the rug to a protective board and applied a paper dust cover to the back.

Although this is the first time Linda's work has appeared in *Celebration*, her daughter Jessica Ford was a finalist in *Celebration XVII*.

LINDA POWELL
NAVARRE, OHIO

Linda was introduced to rug hooking by her mother-in-law, and she hooked her first rug in 1988. She has hooked over 30 rugs and about the same number of small projects. A McGown Certified Instructor, she serves as the current director of the Southern McGown Teachers Workshop. She teaches at her home-based studio and has taught for guilds and rug camps. Some of her designs are available through Honey Bee Hive Rug Hooking. She dyes her own wool and occasionally sells it as Village Rim Rug Hooking. Three of her small "challenge" pieces have taken ribbons in McGown National Exhibits.

Gartenstraße (Garden Street), 25" x 19" without frame, 30½" x 24½" with frame, #3-cut on linen. Designed and hooked by Linda Powell, Navarre, Ohio, 2014. GLEN KERNS

In the Judges' Eyes

- *A warm and inviting piece; particular appreciation of the way that the many panes in the door glass and the window were hooked—great!*

Ghost Trees

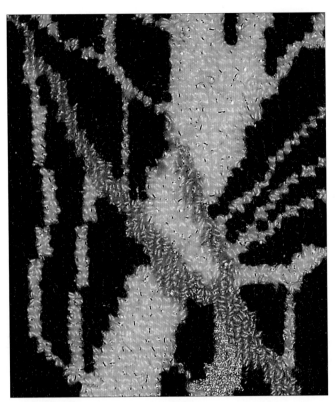

"The design comes from one of several photos I took while sitting beside a campfire late one night in Algonquin Park. We were shining a light up into the tree branches over our heads to fool my camera into taking flash pictures. The stark whites and exaggerated perspectives that I captured were like catching glimpses of the hidden bones of the forest. I realized that, quite by accident, I had finally unlocked what I had been trying to capture while studying dead forests along the Newfoundland shores years before."

Karen Miller did no dyeing for this work. "Although using pre-dyed wool limits my palette, it has not yet limited my expression. When it does, and when my young children are a little older and I have a little more time, I will pursue this further. This piece was hooked entirely using new yarns, sari ribbon, and metallic yarns."

The most significant challenge in this design "was removing the unnecessary complexity of the real forest and reducing the structure to a clean and striking design. Choosing to mimic the clarity of the original photo and work in black and white also meant I had to carefully plan my contrasting elements. To resolve these challenges, I modelled my design after the technique sketch artists use to quickly establish recognizable images with only a handful of hurried baseline strokes."

Once the idea was planned, "it only took about two months to hook and frame it. The hooking itself is clean, incorporating long runs of identical values to emphasize the underlying structure."

Karen's favorite part of the piece "is the distorted perspective, which I tried to stretch even further by using a relatively tall, narrow layout. The trees seem to arch into a towering cathedral ceiling, and the fading grey tones hint at more giants standing hidden beyond the flash."

This rug was exhibited at *Colors Caught in Fibre: Rug-Hooking Made Modern* in Niagara-on-the-Lake, Ontario and *Celebrating Color in Fibre* in Toronto, Ontario—two independent exhibitions put on by previous *Celebration* finalists from Ontario.

Karen prefers to work small-scale, "usually between 12 and 36 inches in length. I have also done many postcard-sized scenes from my family travels. My style is changing. *Ghost Trees* is an important piece for me because it represents my departure from faithfully reproducing what I see, and listening more to what I feel."

KAREN MILLER
OTTAWA, ONTARIO, CANADA

Karen is a self-taught rug hooker who began rug-hooking in 2008 with a kit she found in Cheticamp, Nova Scotia. She has hooked more than 40 pieces. A member of the Green Mountain Rug Hooking Guild, she sells her work in Corner Brook, Newfoundland, and through exhibitions. This is her third appearance in Celebration, her second as a finalist. Her piece Solitude was awarded a Viewer's Choice Award at Hooked in the Mountains in Shelburne, Vermont, in 2012.

Ghost Trees, 17" x 32", wool and metallic yarn and silk sari ribbon on rug warp.
Designed and hooked by Karen Miller, Ottawa, Ontario, Canada, 2014. DANIEL MACDONALD

Leo's London

Mary Ellen Wolff's grandson, Leo, was born in London; he turned four this year. "I wanted to hook a rug with roads, train tracks, and an airport, and to give him every scenario I could think of for match-box sized cars and trucks, along with major landmarks around London."

Mary Ellen sketched out a plan of the rug and sent it to her son and daughter-in-law for approval and more ideas. "I included Buckingham Palace, Kensington Palace, the Museum of Natural History (that dinosaur is in the front lobby), Big Ben, Heathrow Airport, St. Mary's Hospital (where Leo was born), Leo's home, and various other establishments: a pub, fish and chips eatery, ice cream shop, petrol station and 'Grammy's Taco Truck' (tacos are my specialty). I also used artistic license by including our farm here in Northwest Washington. I located it across the road from Buckingham Palace (I don't think the Queen would be pleased!)."

For the colors, she dyed and over-dyed "in a big, open pot, stirring constantly for a minimum of mottling. I used 100 percent wool, new and used. I used solids for the buildings and many other textures (plaids, checks, and herringbones) for interest."

Leo's London was "very fun" to hook. The challenge was "to fit in everything that I wanted and also to tackle all those buildings with so *many* windows in a #2-cut! It took me a little over a year to hook. I finished the rug by whipping the edge with wool yarn."

Leo's family has now moved to Brooklyn, where Leo plays on the rug in his room.

Lessons learned?

"I learned that no amount of work is too much to spend on a beloved family member (although I already knew that)!"

MARY ELLEN WOLFF
FERNDALE, WASHINGTON

Mary Ellen holds a bachelor's degree in graphic design, and her jobs included that of art director of the RMS Queen Mary Ocean Liner in Long Beach, California. "If there is one thing that stands out in my world of art and designing anything, it is the importance of creating good design." She turned to rug hooking in 1996 and formed a group that still meets. She has hooked many rugs and wall hangings, has taught classes at three ATHA Biennials, and sells original patterns for rug hookers on Etsy. Her business name is Sunnybrook Design. This is her first appearance in Celebration.

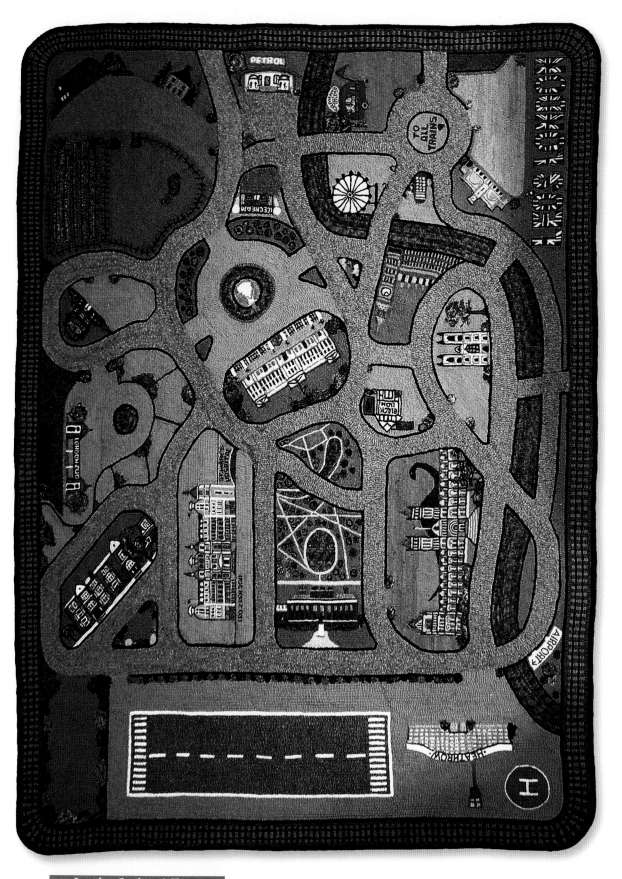

Leo's London, 65" x 50", #2-, 3-, 4-, 6-, and 8-cut wool on monk's cloth.
Designed and hooked by Mary Ellen Wolff, Ferndale, Washington, 2014. THOMAS J. MOELLER

In the Judges' Eyes

• *Very original; love the train track border and London theme; it will be the absolute best thing for Leo, whoever the lucky guy is!*

Letting Go

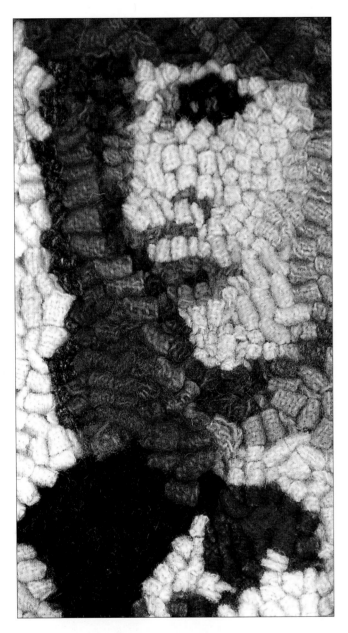

dreams, color, and humanity; something I read in the news or a book; something someone says."

Her grandmother was a great artistic influence in her life. "She taught me how to paint, which is something I still enjoy." Her family is also very supportive "and are, thankfully, oblivious to the wool dust."

Cheryl had made the sketch behind this work while she was thinking about how difficult it is for people to let go. "The soldier came later."

She used 100 percent new wool for the project, some as-is but much of it hand-dyed: dip dye, spot dye, and color overlay. "My challenge was to use a dip dye in the upper sky and spot dyes for the clouds." The rug took about four months to complete.

"It is funny, but when I teach I discourage ripping out. I am thinking there is always a way to salvage what is already there. When I am hooking, I rip out willy nilly. If it does not suit me, then out it comes."

Cheryl likes to hang her works-in-progress where she can see them as she is working on the computer. She redid several things in this rug.

"I have a journal that records the changes I make in a rug. Sometimes it is only three stitches and other times it may be an entire motif. The biggest challenge in this rug was to make the child look like a child."

She finished the rug by trimming and zigzagging the edges, rolling the linen to the front, then basting and whipping the edge with Ryegarn yarn.

She enjoys watching people encounter the rug for the first time "as they scan it and realize the story that it tells."

"*L*etting Go is an idea that started out as a sketch of a mom and a little girl, with the idea of the mother letting go and allowing the child more freedom. As the idea jelled, I began to think of the project in layers of meaning. I like to create in a collage-like manner and want the story to slowly unfold as a person looks at the rug. Concepts that include common human experiences attract me."

Cheryl Bollenbach is a sculptor who works in clay, concrete, wood, and assemblage. "The human figure is often the subject of my work. Inspiration comes from anywhere—

CHERYL BOLLENBACH
GOLDEN, COLORADO

Cheryl started rug hooking in 2005 and has hooked more than 40 rugs. She is a McGown Certified Instructor and teaches classes in her home dye studio. She is the current editor for ATHA magazine and director of South Central McGown Teachers Workshop. This is the second appearance of her work in Celebration.

Letting Go, 51" x 41", #3- to 9-cut wool on linen. Designed and hooked by Cheryl Bollenbach, Golden, Colorado, 2014.

- *Beautiful, moving interpretation of a very sad emotion, high impact from the subject matter; lots to consider for the viewer.*

Little Bear

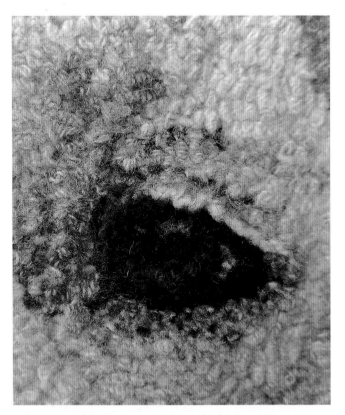

Ever since she completed a couple of animals in smaller cuts in classes with Judy Carter and Jon Ciemiewicz, Therese Shick was eager to hook a realistic rug of her dog, Bear. "I started the rug in a class at the Hunterdon County Guild summer camp, taught by the amazing Judy Carter, in August 2013 and finished it in January 2014."

Most of the wools in this rug are as-is, "and I learned from Judy that these types of wools give the most realistic animal details."

One particular challenge of the rug was hooking the flop on the left ear. "I was initially struggling with getting the ear to look right and then I remembered one of the things Judy Carter taught us in the class. She always stressed, 'Hook what you see.' So I took the photo and just concentrated on that area, not thinking of what it should look like, but just what the photo showed me. I didn't step back from the ear until I was done, and, amazingly, it looked pretty good. The other area that was challenging was the monochromatic color of Bear. I tried to gather enough different values of creams to be able to create some depth."

Therese likes the eyes best. "It took me a couple of tries until I felt that they were right. My son, Rob, who is a graphic designer, was really helpful when I was struggling." The rug is bound with cording and whipped yarn.

Initially Therese was drawn to wider cuts and hooked primarily primitive rugs. "Over time I became more interested in finer cuts with the corresponding level of shading and detail that they can accomplish. Now I really enjoy all cut widths for the different effects that each width can bring."

Although she "absolutely loves" to dye her own wool, "I continue to learn that it is possible to hook with as-is wools cut in #3s and #4s." With this piece, she was reminded that, "when it comes to hooking realistic animals, it's important to 'hook what I see' from the visual aid; and that having a wide range of values of the same color gives more possibilities for depth."

She has hooked probably 100 items or so (rugs, pocketbooks, 3D objects) in the nine years since she began.

"Like many other rug hookers, I have always been involved with other crafts. But somehow rug hooking really spoke to me and took hold."

THERESE SHICK
ANNANDALE, NEW JERSEY

Theresa took her first class at a New Jersey art museum class taught by current ATHA president Gail Dufresne. "I had always wanted to try it, so this was the perfect chance. With Gail as inspiration, I was definitely 'hooked.'" She loves designing her own patterns, but she also hooks commercially available patterns. "There are lots of fabulous patterns out there." She is a member of the Lamb Yankees ATHA Chapter, Hillsborough, New Jersey, and co-president of the Hunterdon County Rug Artisans' Guild, Flemington, New Jersey.

In the Judges' Eyes

- *Delicious combinations of white, gray, cream, and pinky-golds; soulful eyes and regular expression; such character and personality, with outstanding textural details!*

Little Bear, 19″ x 27″, #3- to 5-cut wool on rug warp.
Designed by Leonard Feenan and hooked by Therese Shick, Annandale, New Jersey, 2013.

Memories

the old stone house: the gazebo where I had my 50th birthday, the pet ducks my boys raised, Ferman the pet pygmy goat, and the wonderful old yellow rag-top Karmann Ghia. Both of my boys learned to drive stick-shift in that car and took their dates to the prom in it as well. The car looked even better in the drawing, as rust was the only thing holding it together in the end."

Once the design was in hand, "enter Cindy Irwin, my teacher," who assisted with color planning and "getting the perspective over all the lines of the rug." Joining the roof was a particular challenge for Vickie.

Cindy also contributed "beautiful over-dyed wool" and, most of all, "her patience with a #8-cut rug hooker transforming into a #3- and #4-cut hooker. All of you wide-cuts will certainly understand. There is not enough chocolate to soothe those times. Looking back at the undertaking of such a large project in a #3 cut, I realized there is a rug-hooking fairy for each of us #8 hookers to guide, suggest, and plan."

This rug has been "a wonderful, emotional, and sometimes weepy—but oh so satisfying—return on my labor. Seasons may change, but our rugs allow us to experience the sense of all the seasons right before our eyes."

Lessons learned: "Eat lots of chocolate and go for the #3 cut. It's so worth it. Let your imagination be your own."

"We had finally decided to sell our 105-year-old stone home after living there for 34 years. Downsizing is not something you take a college course to prepare for."

Vickie Landis started rooting through and unpacking all the things she'd kept for years, "just in case the boys want this." The boys are now 43 and 46. "I never realized the whirlwind of memories that would come along with each box—report cards, award certificates, Cub Scout pins—all saved with the idea that they might want to see these things again."

After they moved, Vickie's husband suggested the she hook the old house. "That sounded like a wonderful project, so I collected many photos from the past and sent them off to artist Leonard Feenan. These photos were snapshots of moments from our lives: birthdays, getting ready for a high school dance, playing with pets in the yard."

What she got back "was a true piece of art, combining these moments into a single frame that captures our lives in

VICKIE LANDIS
MOUNT JOY, PENNSYLVANIA

Vickie first encountered rug hooking about 10 years ago when she saw a woman in an antique shop hooking a small Santa. She immediately started researching, found a copy of Celebration *featuring the home of Rebecca Erb, got directions to her place—got lost—and persevered until she found her. Then, one summer, a friend asked if she would like to sit and hook on this "wonderful wraparound porch" at a home in Mt. Gretna. That was her introduction to her current teacher, Cindy Irwin. Vickie has completed "maybe 15 pieces," all rugs. They hold lots of memories and will probably be passed on to her two boys and five grandchildren who already have their eyes on them. "I never thought when I bought that copy of* Celebration *that I would be in it."*

Memories, 41" x 33", #3- and 4-cut spot-dyed and overdyed wool on monk's cloth. Designed by Leonard Feenan and hooked by Vickie Landis, of Mount Joy, Pennsylvania, 2014. IMPACT XPOZURES

In the Judges' Eyes

- *The use of simple and common subjects tell a unique story; pretty color palette, good hooking skills, enjoyable contrast between the old house and the brighter, more modern automobile, great animals; like the hit-or-miss grass.*

My Friend Willie

The wool for this rug came from Janice Lee, of Black Horse Antiques and Rug Hooking. "The only part I needed to work on was Willie's sweater, which need to be in shadow on one side. I used tea to darken the wool."

Two teachers have shaped Mary Jo's artistic vision "and caused me to go out of my box. One is Pris Buttler, who is so encouraging, and the other is Donna Hrkman, who always knows where to put the shadows and colors to use for the shading."

Mary Jo's favorite parts of the rug are the eyes and glasses. "I thought the glasses would be hard to do, but they went in right away. Donna Hrkman helped me with the eyes." Mary Jo added the flag in the background, "as Willie is very patriotic."

The rug took "longer than usual, as most of it was fine cut. I will say four months. I also had to take out some of the shadowing I thought was too dark."

Challenges: The hair. "The color in the picture is more gold than Willie's hair is in real life, as the sun was shining on her when I took the picture." Donna offered some tips here, and on other areas, as well.

"By hooking this rug, I gained a great deal of knowledge about shading. Donna would say, 'Place an area about an inch around the shadow side and make the flag darker in that area.' I know that I would not have thought of that, and I know I won't forget it."

"Willie is one of those people everyone loves." While visiting designer and author Maggie Bonanomi in Missouri, Mary Jo Lahners took this photo of her friend Willie, a "one-of-a-kind" person who is responsible for, among other things, the "Willie's Underwear" project in Lincoln, Nebraska.

"While Willie was on the school board, after retiring from teaching, she realized that many of the children were wearing wet clothing on days that it rained, or if they had had accidents. She started collecting underwear and taking things to the school nurses so the children could be dry all day and not be embarrassed."

Now, the award-winning project includes sweatsuits, underwear, socks, and sometimes shoes: "Our winters are cold and wet, and some children are still wearing sandals." School nurses might also request special items. Willie uses donations to purchase necessities in all sizes, "so that every child has the opportunity to be dry."

MARY JO LAHNERS
LINCOLN, NEBRASKA

A retired elementary school teacher, Mary Jo has been rug hooking for 11 years and has hooked about 100 rugs. She prefers primitives in #8 or #9 cuts, "but I've done lots of dogs and people that take a smaller cut." This is her second work to appear in Celebration. *She is the District 8 Representative for ATHA, and her work has been awarded Best of Show and other awards at the Nebraska State Fair. She tries to hook three hours a day, and meets weekly with a group of hookers who honored her by creating beaded bracelets for themselves: WWMJD (What Would Mary Jo Do?).*

My Friend Willie, 19¹/₂″ x 21″, #5- to 8.5-cut wool on linen.
Drawn on linen by Lou Ann Ayres and hooked by Mary Jo Lahners, Lincoln, Nebraska, 2014. DAVID DALE

In the Judges' Eyes

- *Poignant image in a dynamic angle with original choice of flag background; raises interest about the story behind the image.*

Over the Moon

While attending Sauder Village in 2013, Deb Szwed learned that the theme challenge for 2014 was "On the Move." As she browsed gift books for her grandchildren, "the cow jumped over the moon" came to mind. "Wouldn't that be fun to do? All the way home in the car I was thinking of possibilities. How could I pull this off?"

"My teacher, Jan Frank, dyed the sky and moon wool for me. I wanted it to be a night sky, so I thought the wool with

the silver metal flecks would give the illusion of stars. She dip dyed the flecked wool to obtain the gradual color change, and I hooked the strips in the order that they were cut. The challenge for her was to dip dye a 36" x 60" piece of wool! Needless to say, her arms took quite a beating."

Jan also spot dyed the yellow for the moon to suggest "the man in the moon" and the mottled look of the moon's surface. "The white fence was hooked from recycled winter white wool dyed with pennies to reduce its starkness. The wool from the barn was off-the-bolt wool overdyed to soften the contrast." The rope for the tire swing is embroidery floss.

From concept to completion the work took about nine months; however, it only took about a month to actually hook.

"What took the greatest amount of time was getting the vision for the mechanism that was in my head explained to my mechanical wizard of a friend who made the mechanical component for me."

And the greatest mechanical challenge was "the arc. The path that the cow traveled had to be just right so she actually did jump over the moon and land on the base level and soft."

In terms of lessons, "I learned about value. For the night scene the values had to be dark enough to allude to night but light enough to be able to discern the detail."

Deb's favorite part of this piece is that "it is not traditional rug hooking. I enjoy seeing how pixelated it looks close up and how it all blends together with a little distance. And, of course, I love the fact that it moves. The piece is on display in my living room. My grandson enjoys flipping the switch when he comes over to visit."

Over the Moon, 20" x 7" x 18", #5- and 8-cut wool on unbleached linen, wood, and metal. Mechanism by Dave Morphy; woodworking by Bob Krespan; designed, hooked, and assembled by Deb Szwed, Taylor, Michigan, 2014. JOHN ANGUS

In the Judges' Eyes

- *What a wonderful idea! Natural color palette keeps this piece out of the "cute" category and in the "delightful" arena; outstanding originality, each and every detail is perfect; very fun piece.*

DEB SZWED
TAYLOR, MICHIGAN

Deb began rug hooking about three years ago after observing the president of the local rug-hooking guild hooking at a knit-in. She has hooked 12 rugs. The first, a companion rug to a quilt, won the Sauder Award in 2013. This work won the People's Choice award in the theme challenge "On the Move" at Sauder Village in 2014. Deb is a member of ATHA, the Ontario Hooking Craft Guild, and the McGown Guild's Michigan Rugg Artistes in Dearborn. She has started the process to become a McGown Certified Instructor.

Pearls of Wisdom

*Pearls of Wisdom, 53" x 22¹/₂", #3- to 8-cut wool and metallic yarn on linen.
Designed and hooked by Capri Boyle Jones, Navarre, Florida, 2014.*

"Pearls are my favorite jewelry. Mother gave me hers a few years ago. This design developed from a photograph of her pearls on my dresser, reflection included. Classic, simple elegance—nonetheless challenging to fashion in rug hooking." Capri Boyle Jones chose to hook this piece as a study in whites.

"My personal style can best be described as varying degrees of Impressionism. I enjoy all variety of cuts and employ embellishments depending on the desired end result." In this rug Capri used a variety of custom hand-dyed and as-is wool, both new and recycled, and metallic yarn for the findings.

"I am particularly fond of the simple design. Complexity exists in portraying off-white pearls dimensionally. The reflection has its own intricacies. Yet, the completed hooking maintains the original simple elegance."

The owner of Capri Boyle Rug Studio is able to give a pretty good estimate of the amount of time it took to hook: about 120 hours. While it usually hangs in her master bedroom, "the rug has also traveled with me to various business venues. Viewing the rug periodically allows me to continue the study of whites."

Pearls of Wisdom contained two challenging areas: First, how to create a string of off-white pearls with visual interest. "An array of whites and tints were selected for the pearls to create a three-dimensional effect." The second challenge was handling "how each pearl, in relation to the light source, influenced the wooden surface in varying

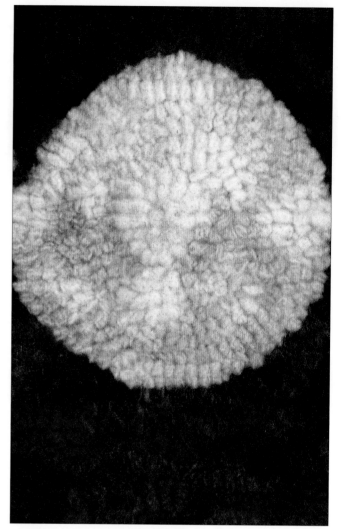

In the Judges' Eyes

- *Unique composition, creative and well done, fantastic background detail; love the upper turquoises and purple, appreciate the effort to capture the shading and the luster of pearls.*

degrees along the strand." While hooking the reflection, Capri returned regularly to the original image for further study.

"The amount of color incorporated into the off-white pearls was considerably reduced upon hooking the dresser, due to the high contrast of dark chocolate and the range of colors in the reflections. Developing the reflection utilized more color and values than I initially thought would be necessary." The rug was finished by whipping the edges with wool yarn coordinated with the adjacent hooked area.

Pearls of Wisdom was selected for a special juried exhibition at Quayside Art Gallery, Pensacola, Florida, where it hung for six weeks.

CAPRI BOYLE JONES
NAVARRE, FLORIDA

Capri began rug hooking 22 years ago through adult education classes with McGown Certified Instructor Genevieve Patterson. Eventually, rug hooking evolved as her business. A member of the National McGown and ATHA guilds, and a McGown Certified Instructor teaching at various public and private workshops, she exhibits in distinctive art shows and is a displaying member and serves on the board of directors at Quayside Art Gallery. This is the fourth appearance of her work in Celebration.

Pig Race

looking straight at me! A little unnerving at first but I quickly decided I loved it."

She re-hooked the center pig's eyes "so that they looked up and over at the viewer. I decided to leave the right pig looking toward the end. A friend pointed out to me that the right pig was coming up from the inside and focused on passing the pigs that had been distracted by the viewer. I hadn't consciously intended this, but sometimes . . . what is right just happens!"

The most challenging part of the rug was the straw background: "There was just so much of it! I twice ran out of yarn, which meant dyeing more yarn and re-hooking to blend in this new yarn. I also did more re-hooking on the straw than any other part of the rug, trying to get the balance of spotty darks right."

Then came the border. "Each row of the border took four hours to hook. The border had 9 rows . . . four and a half days just to do the border!"

Lessons learned were in the dyeing process. First, creating dye formulas from CMYK values "really didn't work as well as I hoped. I also learned that multi-value swatches are very tricky to do if one doesn't use the same amount of yarn for each step of the process. I am very careful with how much yarn I dye. I try not to have too much left over when I finish a project. However, I think in the future, I will dye the same amount of yarn for each step and just live with the extra."

When Nancy Thun learned the theme for Hooked in the Mountains 2014 was "Meet Me at the Fair," she knew she wanted to use this favorite picture from a 1992 Alaska trip.

The dyeing for this project was an experiment. "This was my first attempt at a loose version of multi-value swatches—meaning I dyed only the transitions I needed." She also wanted to try creating formulas from the CMYK (cyan, magenta, yellow, black) percentages she used in Photoshop™. More about that later.

"I had read that when hooking animals or people one should start with the eyes. I did this, starting with the left pig. My intention had been to set the eyes looking around the turn of the fence toward the finish line. When I had hooked all of the eyes, I stepped back and realized that rather than looking toward the finish, the first pig was

NANCY THUN
HOBOKEN, NEW JERSEY

Nancy (a.k.a. Madonnas of Hoboken) is a freelance set and costume designer for the theater, and spent many years as the set designer for a soap opera. She discovered rug hooking at the New York State Craft Fair in 2007 and finally began hooking in 2009—with yarn—after seeing someone at Acadia National Park hooking at a camp store. She has designed and hooked pillows, small purses, and three rugs. She is a member of ATHA and the Green Mountain Rug Hooking Guild. Two of her rugs were exhibited at the 2014 Hooked in the Mountains show. This is the first appearance of her work in Celebration.

Pig Race, 43" x 32", hand-dyed wool yarn on rug warp. Designed and hooked by Nancy Thun, Hoboken, New Jersey, 2014.

In the Judges' Eyes

- *Saw this in person at Hooked in the Mountains; nice liberties with colors, such a great theme rug.*

PRINTS!

"A labyrinth is an ancient design walked for centuries by cultures all over the world for spiritual guidance, good health, peace, quiet or whatever intention the person chooses. We have a seven-path labyrinth in our yard that we created 25 years ago. I always thought it would make a special rug as I knew the 'walls' of the labyrinth could be braided and the paths hooked."

Kris McDermet used a mixture of as-is and hand-dyed wool from Norma Batastini, Nancy Jewett, and Dorr as well as her own hand-dyed wool in her distinctive combination rug that brings together the traditions of rug braiding and rug hooking.

"I love the mixture of prints: both human and not. The blue sneaker is me, as I wear Keds." The footprint in the Teva sandals is for her husband, Stewart. She made one of his toenails green to reference the time years ago when he painted his nail green to entertain a friend's daughter. Elements reflecting the natural life in Vermont include insects, deer tracks, snakes, bird eggs, pine needles, leaves, flowers, "and the list goes on."

The rug took about a year to complete. It will hang in the main hallway of a local hospital for half a year, then move to its permanent home in their bedroom.

"The hooking was just fun and not difficult. Because the designs were on the floor of the forest, I knew that they could be simple, colorful, and give the essence of the bug, plant, or print."

To finish, Kris padded and lined the hooking with wool quilt padding and thin black suiting wool.

Lesson learned: "I should have planned better on how I was going to put it together at the end. It was much harder than I expected."

The rug earned the Sauder Village 2014 Mixed Media People's Choice award and the Green Mountain Rug Hooking Guild Hooked in the Mountains Show 2014 Viewers' Choice award.

In the Judges' Words

- *Delightful, whimsical, and mesmerizing, with braiding adding unique textural quality that takes simple subject matter into the extraordinary; love the idea of this rug.*

PRINTS!, 5′ round, #5- to 7-cut wool on linen.
Designed, hooked, and braided by Kris McDermet, Dummerston, Vermont, 2014. ALBERT KAREVY PHOTOGRAPHY

KRIS MCDERMET
DUMMERSTON, VERMONT

In 1979, while living in Maryland, Kris learned to braid rugs from Isabel Clough and how to hook from Mary Sheppard Burton. When she "heard of some who were putting braid outside of hooking" she quickly needlepointed an oval (she hadn't quite finished her hooking project) and attached 15 rows of braid—"and I was on my way to today." Kris writes, teaches, and designs rugs. She is "a devoted member" of the Green Mountain Rug Hooking Guild, and a member of ATHA and TIGHR, among others. She has developed a love for wet felting, and she exhibits in multimedia shows entitled "Sisters—Paper, Paint, Wool, Silk" with her sister, watercolor artist Lynn Hoeft.

Satu

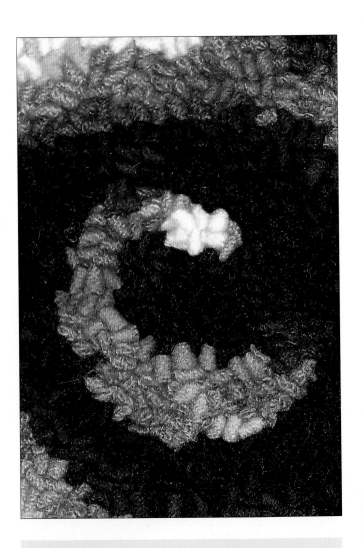

Satu is part of a series called Faces of the Houston Zoo. "It is created from a photo I took of one of the male tigers at the Houston Zoo who prowls around his exhibit."

April DeConick created Satu out of 11 colors in 8-value swatches (or 88 values of 11 colors), that she hand dyed on new white wool. Satu took 144 hours to complete from start to finish ("I kept track").

"The challenge here was the size. It is huge, so I had to map out my pattern very carefully. To keep track of where I was on the image, I used three different color markers when I transferred the pattern to the foundation to delineate light, medium, and dark value zones. This idea worked like a dream. I never got lost as I worked."

In order to create portraits that reveal the essence of the person or animal, April does not try to hook replicas. "I am after the impression." She calls her hooking process "zonalism." She focuses on the light and dark areas of the photo—the value zones. She also has developed a pebbled style of hooking which allows her to blend different wools together seamlessly in her rugs.

"I am intrigued by the use of crazy color in this rug, and how well it works to create an image of the tiger. I wanted to work with greens and grays, to see what they would do in a rug. I tried to push as much green in the rug as it would allow."

The rug was stapled on an oversized gallery wrapped canvas and hangs in April's home. Because of this professional finish, "it looks more like a piece of art" on the wall than a hanging rug.

Lessons learned: "This rug confirmed for me my theories about color and value. I also found that although they are time-consuming, I love to create big pieces because, in the end, they have a presence that smaller mats simply don't. Satu appears life-size, and his presence is very real."

In the Judges' Words

- *Majestic, great expression, outstanding value and color, exciting color choices and combinations; appreciate the slight abstract feel that softens the whole piece; love the eyes.*

APRIL D. DeCONICK
HOUSTON, TEXAS

April is an award-winning hooked wool artist and master dyer. Her work has been featured in Rug Hooking magazine and the ATHA newsletter. This is the third appearance of her work in Celebration. Her pieces earned the Sauder Village People's Choice Awards in 2011, 2012, and 2013. She is a teacher, the author of two books, The Wool Palette *and* Wool Snapshots, *and president of the Stash Sisters ATHA Guild in Region 9. April began hooking in 1995 in rural Michigan at Waterloo Historical Farm.*

Satu, 36" x 48", #6-cut, hand-dyed wool on linen. Designed and hooked by April D. DeConick, Houston, Texas, 2014.

Silver Spring Marketplace

Silver Spring, Maryland, where Sarah Province and her husband have lived for 47 years, has a downtown plaza that features, among other things, a year-round farmers' market on Saturday mornings. "In 2011, on a sunny September morning, as we went down to shop, the sun reflected on the colors of the pumpkins, the apples and the tomatoes! It was a feast for the eyes! Luckily I had my camera with me."

From the 65 pictures she took that day, "I made three paper collages and arranged paper cut-outs from my photos, selecting my favorite subjects in the three sections of my design."

The wool came from "my stash from 40 years of rug-hooking, some recycled but mostly purchased." Also, "there was a material called 'Illumination' available years ago that

used silver, copper and gold fabric bonded onto wool, which I stripped to highlight some metal in the hooking."

Her favorite part of the assemblage is the band. As she was looking over her photos, "it caught my eye even more than when I was there. I like the way that they draw the children and provide various instruments to allow them to help with the music. Whenever I look at the center panel, I always smile because of the joy that I see in the children's faces."

The people were the most difficult part of the hooking. "I didn't want to give too much detail but just enough to show what they were doing. I like shading the clothing. Usually three shades of a color will work—light, medium, and dark." And the most tedious part was the details of the fruit and vegetables—"lots of apples and tomatoes!"

- *The strength of line and structural elements and consistency of hooking tie it all together and takes it from "busy" to a little imaginary vacation; takes us right to the market and helps us remember the sights and smells; creative unity of color.*

Silver Spring Marketplace Triptych, 48" x 18" overall; left and right panels 12" x 18"; center 24" x 18"; #3- and 4-cut wool strips and silver "Illumination" strips on linen. Designed and hooked by Sarah Province, Silver Spring, Maryland, 2014.

LLOYD ATOR

Sarah finishes her pictorials with acid-free mat board or rag board glued to artist stretchers. "I sew strips of wool about 4¹/₂" wide to each side of my hooking to cover the frame, then staple the fabric to the inside of the stretchers. Not only does this give me a framed hooking for display and exhibits, but the mat board on the back provides a place for writing the documentation."

This triptych "challenged all of my skills of design, composition, and hooking. It took longer than most of my work, but I have had a great deal of satisfaction in seeing it develop from my original vision to the execution and the completed work."

The rug earned a blue ribbon and special award at the Maryland State Fair.

SARAH PROVINCE
SILVER SPRING, MARYLAND

Sarah's mother had hooked rugs, so Sarah hooked rugs for her own antiques-furnished home while her children were growing up. In 1990, she met Roslyn Logsdon, who inspired her to hook pictorials from old photographs and family memories. She has self-published the book My Story in Hooked Fiber Art, *which includes pictures of all 60 of her hooked pieces as well as several of her mother's. This is the twelfth time her work has appeared in* Celebration.

Steampunk Reverie

"I discovered the artistic style known as steampunk while I was working in scrapbooking. I was intrigued by the motifs and did a lot of research to create my own interpretation."

Donna Hrkman dyed all of the wool for this piece, primarily over Dorr white, using PRO Chem and Cushing acid dyes. She also overdyed a few textures.

"The rug is hooked in wool, with the exception of the trim around her bodice. That is navy grosgrain ribbon, which I gathered with quilt thread and stitched into place."

Donna drew the pattern in 2013 but didn't start hooking until February 2014. It was finished in May.

"The doggoned ostrich feather on her hat was the worst element by far. I drew it in and tried to hook it in the color I thought would work best, but it didn't. I switched colors and tried again but could not capture the look I wanted. I ripped it out—again!—and drew peacock feathers, hooked a couple of those, hated them, and ripped them out. I chose another color, used the original outline of the ostrich feather and that worked—finally. And I really like it!"

Donna's favorite part of the rug: "I love how well her face turned out and the foggy background, but I also like the copper crow and brick wall. I guess you could say I like the whole thing!"

That said, the rug did have its lessons. "I learned a lot

about perseverance and being brave enough to include embellishments. The key to representing steampunk in a rug was to embrace the metallic elements that are intrinsic to that style. I had to figure out which pieces to use, where they should go, and how to attach them."

Like many of Donna's rugs, *Steampunk Reverie* gets rolled up and goes on the road to teaching venues: "I cover her with a large piece of quilt batting to protect the embellishments." The rug won the People's Choice Award at Sauder Village in 2014.

"I want to acknowledge how important *Rug Hooking* magazine has been to me. As a rug hooker, artist, and teacher, *Rug Hooking* magazine has provided inspiration and information that is specific to what I love most. It has also given me a venue to share my work over the years, and helped me gain recognition and respect in my field. It's always an honor to have a rug chosen for *Celebration*."

In the Judges' Eyes

- *Attention to detail, skill level, and obvious amount of work in an outstanding work of art; obvious orginality but also nice connection to popular themes of the day; what an entertaining rug; so many interesting components beautifully hooked; really original, fitting border; love the hooked and real knobs on the pipes.*

DONNA HRKMAN
DAYTON, OHIO

Donna has explored many media, but when she was introduced to rug hooking 14 years ago, she "immediately began drawing my own designs and patterns." After starting with primitive cuts, she "quickly realized that shading and detail were more my style." She is a teacher, the author of Rug Hooker's Companion, *and six of her rugs have received awards at Sauder Village Rug Hooking Week. This is her eighth work to be included in* Celebration.

Steampunk Reverie, 33″ x 43″, #3- to 5-cut hand-dyed wool on cotton linen and metal embellishments attached with sewing and quilting thread, coated wire, and metal brads (no glue). Designed and hooked by Donna Hrkman, Dayton, Ohio, 2014. DAN HRKMAN

Steamy Windows

Lynne searched for lots of reference images of windows "and did a lot of reverse hooking." The project took about six months.

Her favorite element is the "droopy" stalks of corn.

And her lesson: "Not to put a rug away on a top shelf in a paper bag!"

The rug is sewn to a canvas stretcher that was covered in fabric. Lynne used duct tape to cover the staples.

Although she is a McGown Certified Instructor, she no longer teaches structured classes. "I started a hook-in at Ker Place (a house museum in Onancock, Virginia) with Eric Sandberg, and we meet once a month and I do teach newbies then."

"I've been in *Celebration* before and have been rejected more than I've been accepted. You have to keep trying and not let it get you down when you don't make it. I have always felt that the rugs that 'made it' were better than the one I submitted."

Lynne designs most of her own rugs, "but occasionally a commercial pattern will speak to me and I have to buy it." She tries to attend two workshops a year, with different teachers: "There is always something to be learned from everyone."

It's almost impossible to explain "how rug hooking has enriched my life. My mind is filled with new ideas; I have met fabulous, creative people; I am never bored; there is always that 'new' rug to think about. My sense of touch is heightened by the fabrics I use; I'm fortunate to 'play' in the dye pot. It is an amazing art form."

"I consider myself to be a fiber artist who was fortunate to marry my patron 52 years ago."And her "patron" is part of the inspiration for Lynne Fowler's rug. "This design has been stewing for years. I often listen to Tina Turner when I hook. Her song "Steamy Windows" reminded me of the '60s, when my husband and I would park in a cornfield. I knew I had to put it in a rug some day."

The rug was hooked with new wool: spots, "as well as a ton of leftovers. I didn't dye anything special for the rug."

Lynne started the rug in a class at Cape May with Jen Lavoie. "I took it home, put it away, and lost it. I found it after searching for weeks. It was on the top shelf in a paper bag. Yikes!"

Creating the steamy windows in this rug was a challenge.

LYNNE FOWLER
ONANCOCK, VIRGINIA

Lynne picked up the business card from a rug hooker at a county fair for one of her neighbors. "I never expected to do it myself." She started rug hooking in 1996 and now, 100 rugs later, is still learning and trying new things. "I try all cuts and techniques." She has recently taken up Saori weaving. "I thrive on color and fiber and will try almost anything to get the effects I'm seeking." This is her second work to appear in Celebration.

Steamy Windows, 28" x 20", #3- and 4-cut wool on linen. Designed and hooked by Lynne Fowler, Onancock, Virginia, 2014. DAVID HARP

In the Judges' Words

• *Nice movement in cornstalks and tassels, so much to love about this piece; love the story!*

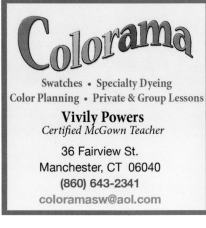

Madison's Fairy

The inspiration for *Madison's Fairy* came during one of Cindy Irwin's own classes, when a student requested a fairy pattern. The class asked Leonard Feenan to design several different patterns, which Lenny gave to Cindy for her catalog.

The face in this piece is a portrait of Cindy's grand-daughter, Madison. Cindy began hooking the face in a class with Laura Pierce: "She made it easy in a #6 cut!"

The turtle image in the rug derives from a family tradition. Each year, the family gathers at a cottage in Michigan, where the annual turtle hunt has become "a highlight of every child's vacation."

Cindy herself dyed almost all of the wool for *Madison's Fairy*, with the exception of the flesh color, which was dyed by Laura Pierce.

Most of the rug is wool, with a small amount of polyester hooked along with wool in the wings. Cuts range from one thread of wool to a #8 cut. The sky and dress are dip-dyed Dorr sparkle wool. Embellishments include pearls in the flowers, crystals as dew drops on the ferns and as stars in the sky, and pyrite on the shore. The rocks are an eight-value Jacobean formula

"The hardest thing was the wings, because I had a preconceived notion that I wanted them to be an alternative material. I hooked them with many different materials, but nothing looked right. I gave up on the alternative materials and hooked them in the lighter shade of the wool used for the sky, so that they look translucent. I added a small amount of polyester to the wool to make them shimmer."

The rug is now on display in Cindy's studio.

Madison's Fairy, 26" x 31", #2- to 8-cut wool and polyester on rug warp, with gemstones. Designed by Leonard Feenan and hooked by Cindy Irwin, of Lancaster, Pennsylvania, 2014.
IMPACT XPOZURES

In the Judges' Eyes

- *Beautiful dress, great ferns, nice gradation of color, with gemstones adding a mystical quality to a sweet story rug.*

CINDY IRWIN
LANCASTER, PENNSYLVANIA

Cindy has been hooking since 1983 and "lost count of the number of rugs completed many years ago." She is a McGown Certified Instructor, teaches in her home studio and at workshops, and is a juried member of the Pennsylvania Guild of Craftsmen. She is assistant director of McGown Teachers Workshop, president of the Conestoga Rug Hooking Guild, Area 2 Rep for ATHA, and chairman of Loanables for the McGown National Guild. This is Cindy's sixth appearance in Celebration.

Norwich

Terryl Ostmo had had her eye on this rug for several years. "After seeing Mary Sheppard Burton's rendition at Sauder Village, done in a #3 or possibly #4 cut, I knew I had to hook my own. Rather than trying to duplicate what Mary had done, I decided I would be more successful developing my own color plan."

Terryl had purchased "a funky red/orange/navy vintage plaid several years ago from Rhonda Manley, of Black Sheep Wool Designs. Also, I had been saving two great bouclés. Those fabrics came together in this rug."

Her favorite part of the rug is in the border. "I think the hit-or-miss really makes the color plan interesting."

Completing the rug, she wrote, "was a breeze. I started it in Sandra Brown's geometrics class at Sauder Village in 2013 and the rug was finished before the end of the year."

Sandra had her students first create a mock-up of their designs in colored pencil. "It was during that exercise that it hit me that I should do hit-or-miss in the outer border. I learned from hooking this rug that it can really pay off to do a colored pencil mock-up on a geometric before diving in with the hooking."

To finish, Terryl folded the backing over cording and whipped with wool yarn. She did not use rug tape.

"In the scroll portion of the pattern, I used both a spot dye and an orange and lavender plaid. That made it a logical decision to use lavender for the leaf accent area in the center. I love how the lavender complements the oranges."

TERRYL OSTMO
WAHPETON, NORTH DAKOTA

When she started hooking in 1998, Terryl was drawn to primitives, but "these days I love every style." She travels each year to the McGown Teachers Workshop in Newton, Iowa, and earned her McGown certification there in 2012. She is a member of the Greater Chicago Area McGown Guild #15 and ATHA.
Her work previously appeared in Celebration XX.

In the Judges' Eyes

• *Very harmonious color palette, unique addition of textures to this pattern, effective use of dark lines and gray lines around feathers and shapes; neutrals add important component.*

Dear Celebration Reader:

Which rugs are your favorites?

The judges have chosen the finalists—now it is up to you to tell us which of these rugs deserve the honor of being named Readers' Choice winners.

Review each of the winning rugs carefully and make your selections. Mark your choices on the attached ballot and be sure to postmark it before December 31, 2015.

RHM appreciates the time you take to send in your Readers' Choice vote. Please help us honor the rug hooking artists represented within the pages of *Celebration XXV* by voting for your choice of the best of the best.

Sincerely,

Debra Smith

Editor

READERS' CHOICE BALLOT

After reviewing all the rugs, fill out this ballot and mail it in to vote. The winners of the Readers' Choice Contest will be announced in the June/July/August 2016 issue of *Rug Hooking* magazine. **Note: Ballots must be postmarked by December 31, 2015.**

MY FAVORITE *CELEBRATION* RUGS ARE:

1ST CHOICE

2ND CHOICE

3RD CHOICE

4TH CHOICE

5TH CHOICE

NAME

EMAIL

☐ Yes, I would like to receive updates from *Rug Hooking* magazine.

Never miss an edition of
CELEBRATION OF HAND-HOOKED RUGS
by joining our RHM *Book Club*

Yes! I want to make sure I never miss an edition of *Celebration of Hand-Hooked Rugs*. Please sign me up for your risk-free *RHM* Book Club. I understand each time a new **Rug Hooking** book is published it will be automatically shipped to me; this includes the annual edition of *Celebration of Hand-Hooked Rugs*. Each book will be mine to examine for 21 days. If I like what I see, I'll keep the book and pay the invoice. If I'm not delighted, I'll return the book at *Rug Hooking* magazine's expense, and owe nothing.

NAME

ADDRESS

CITY/STATE/ZIP   PHONE NUMBER

EMAIL ADDRESS

BCELB15

RUG HOOKING MAGAZINE
5067 Ritter Rd.
Mechanicsburg, PA 17055-6921

Subscription Department
PO Box 2263
Williamsport, PA 17703-2263

Subscription Department
PO Box 2263
Williamsport, PA 17703-2263

Norwich, 54" x 31", #6- to 8-cut wool on monk's cloth.
Designed by Lib Callaway and hooked by Terryl Ostmo, Wahpeton, North Dakota, 2013.

Peacock

Mary Gordon chose this design "because I was intrigued by its complexity, and it was so far outside of my comfort zone that it would be a challenge to interpret."

She purchased the pattern in the spring of 2007 but did not start color planning until the fall of 2009. "I had gotten as far as dyeing the wool and hooking some of the center before I made the decision to attend the Northern McGown Teachers Workshop. This project was set aside while I worked on certification submissions and other projects—not even looking at it again until the winter of 2012. This hiatus turned out to be a blessing, because I was able to look at the design with fresh eyes and apply lessons and new techniques learned during that time. With a small amount of reverse hooking, and enthusiasm, I completed the rug in May of 2014: seven years from purchase to last loop."

She used seven 8-value swatches, and two spot dyes to complete the design. "I dyed the swatches over Dorr Natural and Camel, the bright spot over Woolrich Mona Gray, and my favorite black background over Dorr Olive."

The most challenging part of hooking this rug "was keeping the outer edge visually round." Mary managed this by "looking at, and photographing it on the floor—a lot. The personal challenge I tasked myself with was using the swatch values equally." She alternated the color values between motifs (i.e., 1-3-5-7, or 2-4-6-8), except for the daisies and outer "feathers," where she used eight values of the same color. She finished the rug with a herringbone stitch in a blend of black yarn.

"While hooking this rug, I learned that it is okay for a 'master plan' to be revised, and that I need to challenge myself to continue to improve and evolve as an artist."

Her favorite part of the rug? "The satisfaction that came with its completion."

In the Judges' Eyes

- *Gorgeous color palette, interesting lights and darks, good use of sparkly pink and turquoise together with primitive colors, skillful shading on all elements, with color drawing your eye to the center; love the detail as well as the overall impact.*

This rug was awarded the Mason-Dixon Guild Ribbon at the 2014 Maryland State Fair, and "will be on the floor in my living room as soon as my son's dog is no longer a 'temporary' resident—LOL. (I have been informed for several years that it could be any day!)"

Peacock, 37″ round, # 3-cut wool on linen.
Designed by Harry M. Fraser Company and hooked by Mary H. Gordon, Street, Maryland, 2014. IMPACT XPOZURES

MARY H. GORDON
STREET, MARYLAND

Mary began hooking as a creative outlet in 2001 with the help of a few "how to" books. In 2006, she attended her first workshop, where she arranged to begin study with Peggy Hannum. "Under Peggy's tutelage, I was taken to 'the dark side' (as my dear friend Patti Stone would say), exploring the nuances of fine shading and dyeing techniques." Mary became a McGown Certified Instructor in 2013 and belongs to the Conestoga and Woolwrights guilds. This is her first appearance in Celebration.

Persian Palm

knowledge of repairing hooked rugs, which I continue to do today."

Nancy Beech, from whom Stephanie received the rug, had lived in Burlington, Vermont, "and was a student of my mother in the early 1990s. She started the rug but was unable to finish it, so she sent it to me to complete."

Stephanie "had a sense of what the color plan was supposed to be" because Nancy had included dyed wool and formulas, and there were some markings on the pattern.

Still, "matching the colors was a challenge, given the fact that the Dorr wool that was originally used in overdyeing is not available anymore. I had to dye to match the original color, then overdye to match to specific colors in the rug." To produce enough wool for the project, Stephanie used the open pot method to "dye by eye."

"Also challenging was matching Nancy's hooking technique so that there is no distinguishable difference throughout the whole rug."

The rug took about a year to complete. It was exhibited at Hooked in the Mountains in October 2014, where it received the Viewer's Choice Award. Today, "Nancy proudly displays the rug in her home in Florida."

Lessons learned, even after a lifetime of hooking?

"That I'm not interested in hooking #3-cut strips again."

Stephanie Allen-Krauss received this rug, partially completed, from a member of her guild who had moved to another state a number of years ago. And the guild connection is only part of their shared history.

"Rug hooking has always been a part of my life. From an early age, my mother, Anne Ashworth, started me on small projects. Then, through my teenage years she taught me about dyeing wool, and later, in my 20s, she shared her

In the Judges' Eyes

- *Harmonious color palette, beautiful technique, beautiful overall impact, well balanced, subtle color variations add to the richness; outstanding piece.*

STEPHANIE ALLEN-KRAUSS
MONTPELIER, VERMONT

A fourth-generation rug maker and custom dyeing specialist, Stephanie Allen-Krauss and her family have owned Green Mountain Hooked Rugs since 1982. Stephanie discovered from her dad that his grandmother was a rug hooker, designer, and shop owner. "I've had fun using my great grandmother's stamping blocks and have felt inspired each time I touch them." In the last 15 years, she has hooked over 200 rugs for family and friends and created many commissioned rugs. In 2010 she was honored with the Governor's Award for Best Traditional Artist of the Year in Vermont. She is a member and past treasurer of TIGHR, and past vice president of the Green Mountain Rug Hooking Guild.

Persian Palm, 70" x 105", #3-cut wool on monk's cloth.
Designed by Pearl McGown and hooked by Stephanie Allen-Krauss, Montpelier, Vermont, 2014. ANNE-MARIE LITTENBERG

Poppies Galore

In 2013, Kelly McMahon-Goldstein happened to be visiting her son in North Carolina during Eric Sandberg's Caraway Rug Camp. "Naturally, I went shopping and just fell in love with Carol Kassera's *Poppies Galore* rug design. I was a bit daunted by its size, but purchased it on the spot."

She wanted to begin this rug using only her "snarls" but wasn't sure how. Her "kindred spirit" Gayle Soileau scheduled Eric to teach at her rug camp in Baton Rouge, and Kelly signed up.

"The first day of class, I threw my color-sorted snarl bags on the floor for Eric's critique. Using his familiar stick, he pointed to each bag: 'Dull.' 'Dull.' 'Dull.' Oh my gosh! This was off to a bad start!"

Still, using the available wool, "Eric picked a flower for me to begin with, and I was off." Then, "with a close friend in hand," Kelly went shopping for some brights.

She started on the second poppy, and "midway through, I was ready to toss it in! I can't describe how shocking these brights were to my sensibilities. I was outside my comfort zone for sure. I was dismayed, but with Eric's encouragement, I continued to plod through and finish the second flower."

Kelly worked on the rug one flower at a time. "The challenge for me was that I had always planned to make each flower different but still have their colors harmonize. Once home, for each flower, I pulled snarls from my dull stock and combined them with the new brights I had

purchased. This is when I began to fall in love with the rug."

The leaves were the easiest to hook, apart from the background. "For the leaves, I value swatch-dyed seven different combinations of green. I sorted the greens, not by their color swatch, but more or less by their approximate value. For the background, I gathered various reds, blues, and greens from my stash and overdyed them all with black."

Kelly used half-inch cording and yarn dyed to match the background to whip the edge. "I don't use binding tape on the back of my rugs any longer."

She began the rug in February 2014 and completed it in August 2014.

"I've taken many classes over the years and have heard many teachers say that good color planning should be based on combinations of bright, dull, light, and dark colors. I have also been taught that value is more important than actual color."

KELLY MCMAHON-GOLDSTEIN
PRAIRIEVILLE, LOUISIANA

In 2008, Kelly, then a quilter, bought a book featuring quilt motifs hooked into a rug. With no rug hooking contacts, "I went online and bought Gene Shepherd's The Rug Hooker's Bible. With Gene's book in hand, I bought a cutter, frame, wool, dye, etc. online, drew my first pattern based on another motif in the quilt appliqué book, and I was off to the races. I was determined and committed. Go big or go home." She has hooked about 15 rugs. This is her first rug to appear in Celebration.

Poppies Galore, 66″ x 41″, *mainly #7-cut wool on monk's cloth.*
Designed by Carol Kassera and hooked by Kelly McMahon-Goldstein, Prairieville, Louisiana, 2014.

Pumpkin Thyme

This design by Lori Brechlin has been a favorite of Karen Buchheit since she first started hooking. She began actually hooking it at the 2013 Cedar Lakes Rug Camp with Cindi Gay.

"The blue texture that I used for the background was my favorite blue that year." Cindi suggested using it. "I'd not seen this color used for background in this design." In another innovation, Karen hooked the background in a pattern of small circles to add interest.

"The entire rug was hooked with as-is textures, except for the leaves of his exquisite boutonniere."

Other than his "fabulous boutonniere and striped suit coat," another unique element in this rug is the watch that the pumpkin is holding. From the beginning, Karen wanted to use a real watch instead of hooking one. "My husband and I shopped at a Louisville antique mall and found this broken stopwatch, which is the perfect shape! Then I found a short, antique silver chain that suspends the watch from his hand. He's so very dapper!"

In terms of the rug's most challenging elements, "I wouldn't call it a true challenge," but it took some pondering to figure out "how to make the berries at the top of the two 'stalks' more dimensional than flat. I solved this by bringing up the berry wool strip from the backside in two adjacent holes. Then I tied three knots, each one on top of

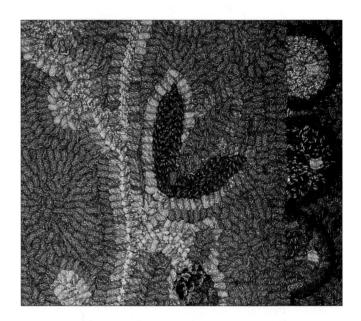

the previous one, pulled the ends back down through to the backside, clipped the ends, and hand stitched them together so they wouldn't migrate back to the front. They definitely have a berry shape now."

Karen finished the rug using "Wendy Miller's corded rug binding technique. I knew he'd never be displayed on the floor, so I thought this wool and cording method would finish him nicely. I used the same textured wool on the binding as in the very outer edge of hooking. I use this method on about 50 percent of my rugs."

She had so much fun hooking this rug that it only took three months to complete. "*Pumpkin Thyme* is displayed in our home year round: He's my husband's favorite rug!" It also won Best in Show in its category at the 2013 Kentucky State Fair.

Lessons learned: "I learned that you can use 'props' in your rug (the watch) if appropriate!"

KAREN J. BUCHHEIT
LOUISVILLE, KENTUCKY

In 2007, Karen started doing punchneedle and "about a year later I had a 'lightbulb' moment while seeing some beautiful antique hooked rugs at a local antique fair. I realized that I could learn how to hook rugs—punchneedle on a grander scale! Jyl Clark, owner of Cathouse Rugs, in New Albany, Indiana, was my first teacher; not a day goes by that I don't at least think about hooking. I've hooked about 20 rugs since early 2009." A member of ATHA and Buffalo Trace Rug Hookers, she now sees the world "through 'hooker's eyes', gathering inspiration for rug designs everywhere I go." Her husband, Greg, has "a keen eye for color" and has helped with many of her wool choices.

In the Judges' Eyes

- Great theme rug with unique take on traditional Halloween colors, nice light outlining, and tiny textural touches that add the whimsy necessary to keep theme rugs alive and happening; love the embellishments in a delightful overall composition.

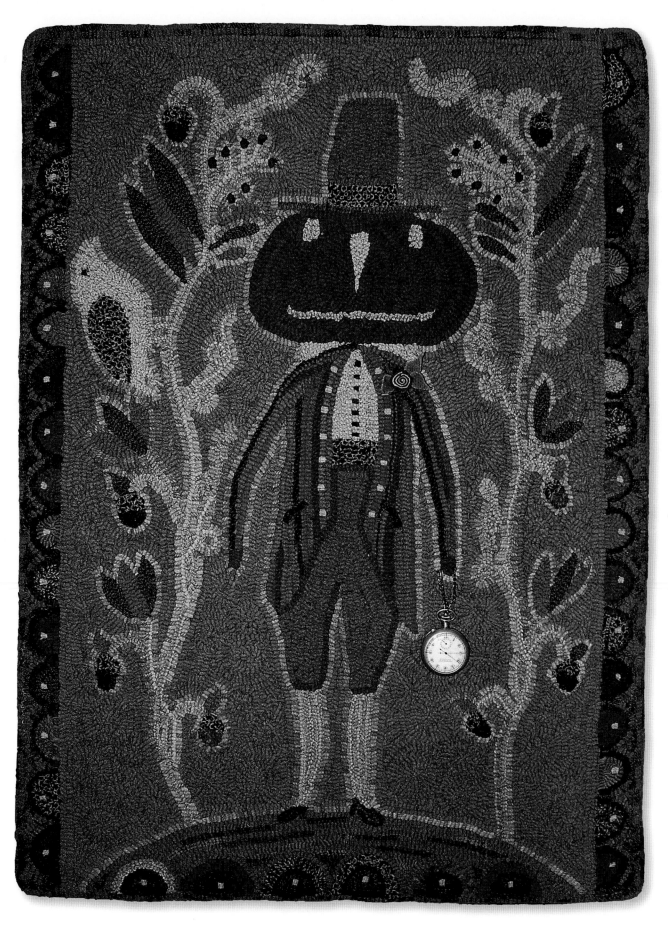

Pumpkin Thyme, 25¹/₂″x 34¹/₂″, #8 and 8.5-cut wool on linen.
Designed by Lori Brechlin and hooked by Karen J. Buchheit, Louisville, Kentucky, 2013.

Royalty

A library book first introduced Lisa Rueger to rug hooking, and she "decided to learn" the technique. How? Well, by flying "back East" from California to meet and study with the author. After that, she continued her studies with teachers and rug camps.

"I was blessed to work with Helen Connelly on this rug. She taught me swatches and dip dyeing."

Lisa started this rug 14 years ago, choosing the design because she loves flowers. Her favorite elements are the the roses and tulips because of their colors.

"The floral design of this rug was completed 14 years ago. I then put the rug away because I was unsure how to develop the scroll."

A couple of years ago, she decided to pull the rug out and tackle it. She successfully developed the scroll—the most challenging part—and pulled the loops higher for the flowers so that they would appear raised and three-dimensional.

The rug is now in the entryway of Lisa's home.

Lisa has completed six rugs to date, and this is her second in *Celebration*. The rug in *Celebration VIII* was also a Pearl McGown design, *Chilcott Leaves*. One of her rugs was also featured on the cover of the ATHA newsletter.

In the Judges' Eyes

• *A beautiful new interpretation of an old pattern, colors so harmonious and technique so skillful; great care and thoughtful hooking very obvious; so many beautiful parts to this rug; even the background sings.*

LISA RUEGER
SIMI VALLEY, CALIFORNIA

Lisa Rueger's first Celebration *appearance was in the 1998 edition, when she was regularly attending the Asilomar and Cambria Pines rug camps. A member of the California First and Orange Coast Classic rug hooking groups, she also enjoys knitting, needle arts, and jewelry making.*

Royalty, 60″ x 36″, #3- and 4-cut dip-dyed and swatch-dyed wool on monk's cloth.
Designed by Pearl McGown and hooked by Lisa Rueger, Simi Valley, California, 2013.

Swirl

for the United Methodist Church. She recently returned from guiding a group to Israel/Palestine.

"I feel my being drawn to rug hooking is a desire to create something of beauty, a feeling that can be shared here at home as well as around the world, and most recently in a refugee camp in Bethlehem."

For this rug, she used a technique, taught to her by Nancy Blood, of "soaking and dyeing an array of wools together using one formula." This creates a "wonderful" blending and streaking that married the colors for the scrolls. While it took "40 years to get around to it," the rug took "only about two years to dye and hook." Her student Helen Lynch copied the original design from "two pieces of old Angus burlap" onto linen, and Peggy started the rug at Maryland Shores Workshop, where Nancy "provided her expertise for the Jack-in-the-pulpits in the center."

A challenge in this rug was deciding on the background. "I tried several pieces; some caused the colors to 'die.' It needed something reddish to make the scrolls come alive." Her favorite part is "the movement and sense of swampy miasma created through the dyeing."

Like most of her choices of rugs, "the bigger, the better. Somehow, the bigger the rug, the faster it goes, and when I'm done, I have something big *and* spectacular!"

Fiber art is a family legacy for Peggy Hannum. Her grandmother started her own business making drapes and slipcovers, and Peggy sewed doll clothes from the fabric scraps. Peggy started sewing her own clothing in eighth grade, later knitting designer sweaters, creating and sewing couture outfits, and finally, discovering rug hooking by way of "my sewing and knitting buddy, Lyn Lovell."

In the mid-'70s, she and Lyn began collecting Heirloom Patterns, "all on old burlap." Lyn's husband attended school with Bob Zeiser, whose mother, Louise Zeiser, created Heirloom Patterns. "Lyn and I pored over the old Heirloom pattern book like our children devoured the Sears catalogue at Christmas. *Swirl* has been on my shelves that long!"

Peggy has hooked more than 40 rugs and many small pieces, "most of which are fine-cut #3 or #4, shaded with 8-value swatches. However I have ventured into even a #9-cut and enjoyed pushing my comfort zone—but not too often!"

After retiring from teaching high school English, Peggy and her husband accepted positions as Liaisons to Jerusalem

PEGGY HANNUM
LANCASTER, PENNSYLVANIA

As a McGown Certified Instructor, Peggy has been teaching for the last 19 years, officially retiring this year from teaching and as historian for the McGown Guild. While Peggy is deeply grateful to her two teachers and mentors, Meredith LeBeau and Nancy Blood, "my students, who have shared their ideas, expertise, and enthusiasm, have been my most exciting inspiration." Peggy's work has appeared in eight past editions of Celebration, *including the first. Her work was selected for the cover of the 20th Anniversary Edition of Rug Hooking magazine, and her home featured in a series about "Decorating with Hooked Rugs." She has had many award-winning rugs at the annual Gallery Show of the Pennsylvania Guild of Craftsmen.*

Swirl, 59" x 68", #4- and 5-cut hand-dyed new wool on linen.
Designed by Heirloom Patterns and hooked by Peggy Hannum, Lancaster, Pennsylvania, 2014. IMPACT XPOZURES

In the Judges' Eyes

- *Really fabulous representation of the nature of the Jack-in-the-pulpit; complex color palette a unique and courageous jump from traditional colors, full of movement and exuberance; flowing scrolls, dramatic curling leaves.*

Victorian

wool. "A lot of the flowers were hooked with leftovers." She used a combination of navy and plum to get the rich red background. Marion also used spots and 8-value swatches of new Woolrich wools for this piece. For the scrolls, she dyed a selection of colors (natural, pink, blue, violet, and white) "with the same green formula as one of the leaves. It worked well."

She's made 25 pieces, and most of them are large. Her first love is florals. However, she has plans for two "wild" rugs adapted, with permission, from an artist's work she found online. "Everyone's asking me why am I breaking out of my shell."

The biggest challenge in hooking this round rug was "keeping it round and flat." She succeeded with "a lot of being careful and steam pressing." Marion also uses a special finishing technique. After a round rug is hooked, she sews a running stitch around the edge of the rug to ease any distortion, the way a sewer would ease an armhole. She also presses as she goes, which makes it easier to reach all areas of a larger rug.

The rug took about nine months from start to finish, and earned a First Place and Viewers' Choice awards at the Maryland State Fair.

This is a very special issue of *Celebration* for Marion, three other students of Peggy Hannum, and the student of a student of Peggy Hannum: Peggy is retiring this year, and, independently of that fact, her rug was selected as the cover image for this year's book. This year's *Celebration* also includes work by Peggy's students Cindy Irwin, Patricia Levin, and Mary Gordon, and also by one of Cindy's students, Vicki Landis. "We were all so excited and calling each other when we heard."

This rug is one of Marion's favorites. "Some rugs you finish and you say, 'Well, that's nice.' Some are in my closet. This one is out on my floor for people to see."

"Such a pretty rug, how could I not hook it?" Marion Reddy Sachs came to rug hooking after arthritis prevented her from continuing to make her highly respected quilts. But long before that, she had seen a group of women rug hooking at a street fair and thought she might like to try it someday. When her quilting work ended, "I found *Rug Hooking* magazine in a bookstore and took it from there."

Marion has been hooking for about 15 years, and was a student of Peggy Hannum for 12. This rug represents her preferred materials: monk's cloth and #3-cut hand-dyed

In the Judges' Eyes

- *Lovely example of a technically executed McGown Flynn pattern; subtle color palette keeps it from overpowering; vintage look, heirloom quality; background direction and color are great!*

Victorian, 61″ round, #3-cut Woolrich wool on monk's cloth.
Designed by Jane McGown Flynn and hooked by Marion Reddy Sachs, York, Pennsylvania, 2013. IMPACT XPOZURES

MARION REDDY SACHS
YORK, PENNSYLVANIA

Marion is highly regarded for both her quilts and rugs, and her work in both media was highlighted in an episode of the Internet-based Quilters News Network in 2012. Most recently, The Woolwrights Rug Hooking Guild of Lancaster County, Chapter #110 of ATHA, of which she is a member, honored her with a special exhibition of her rugs at its 2015 annual spring hook-in.

Victorian Garden

finish till it was done. I started the rug in August at Capri's house, where we selected wonderfully vibrant wool from Capri's collection. Then, in January at Off the Ocean Rug Camp, Diane Stoffel applied her magical color sense with a few additional enhancements to the original plan." JoAnne admires the way that others "can take your verbal vision" and help make it reality.

She is a member of the North Florida ATHA Rug Hooking Guild, which she has served as secretary and treasurer. She does "one serious rug a year," and she decided to enter this one into *Celebration* because of the comments that people were making as they watched the rug develop. They thought the colors were "stunning" and suggested "it had a chance."

"The scale of the flowers was fun to do"—they are the largest flowers she has ever hooked. On the other hand, "the background seemed to go forever and ever and ever. That did wear on my patience a bit."

JoAnne used #4 and #5 cuts for the flowers. The background—"all three yards of it"—was done primarily in a #6 cut.

Each time she makes a rug, Joanne envisions where she will use it. At the moment, though, all of them are rolled up and stored; the grandchildren, frequent visitors, tend to slide on them.

She uses mostly commercial patterns, but she has designed a turtle rug, ostensibly for the foyer.

"I am very honored to have a rug in *Celebration*."

JoAnne Perrone saw her first rug when co-worker Katie Puckett brought in a rug she was taking to a conference. "This is the only craft I've ever seriously done. It's almost like painting with wool. You have the flexibility and freedom to create a rug of any dimension."

JoAnne loves bright colors, and, when she looks at her rugs together, finds she favors a lot of the same colors: bright orange, bright purple, bright springtime colors. "I'd seen this rug *Victorian Garden* hooked with fine shading and was thrilled when I received the color plan from Capri Boyle Jones with bright vivid colors. I started hooking and didn't

In the Judges' Eyes

• *Really energetic and dynamic piece, sparkly; fabulous composition, exciting color palette, value shading, and contrast.*

JoAnne Perrone
Ponte Vedra Beach, Florida

"I tell everyone I've been rug hooking for 10 years but if I actually checked a calendar it would likely be closer to 15 years. My first teacher was Carol Kassera; I did a wonderful geometric design and have been 'hooked' ever since. Most of my rugs have been large designs with very little fine shading and they almost always include very bright intense colors." This is her first work to be featured in Celebration.

Victorian Garden, 36" x 47", #4- and 5-cut wool on linen.
Designed by Roche Riverhouse Designs and hooked by JoAnne Perrone, Ponte Vedra Beach, Florida, 2014. JOSEPH BAILEY

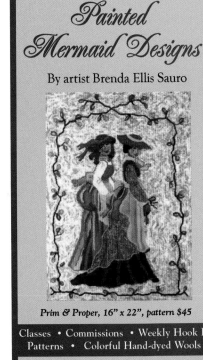

Adaptation of Christian

Christian is the nephew of artist Jodi Isom, and this rug was a gift for his 2014 college graduation in graphic design. The original photo was taken by one of Christian's teachers, who was inspired by the Mohawk haircut. When she saw the photo, Jodi thought, "If I ever wanted to do a portrait, this would be it."

And so it was. She signed up for a workshop with Donna Hrkman to attempt, for the first time, a portrait in small cuts. Jodi made her own pattern: enlarging the photo, outlining the major features, then transferring the design to linen by using red-dot pattern tracing fabric.

The colors? "I decided to do the rug in sepia but wanted to make the Mohawk 'on fire.' My nephew on occasion would dye his Mohawk different colors and I wanted to represent this." With a clear vision of the final work, though, "I was lost on how to start on this rug." Donna advised her to figure out the lightest and darkest parts of the photo first and then fill in.

"The forehead was the lightest part, so I started there and worked around the outside of the face. I then moved on to the ear and earring. This was the most difficult part of the rug because it was hard to keep the image of the earring from disappearing into the ear or neck. Adding a few highlights helped." The beard and hair were hooked with random shades, and she beaded the necklace to create the look of a chain hanging from Christian's neck.

"My favorite part is the Mohawk. It took me a few times to figure out how to capture movement in the flames. Using three different shades of orange and white, I was able to create a realistic effect—it just looked 'fun' to me."

Jodi had originally intended to write a message in the background, but, with Donna's help, decided instead on a radiating circle around the face to express Christian's energy and enthusiasm. She added a simple college logo and his graduation date, then finished the rug with wool yarn.

The portrait took two months, and Jodi learned "how to bring life and personality into a portrait piece by following the natural contours of a face." This rug has also given her the confidence to continue using small cuts.

JODI ISOM
LINCOLN, NEBRASKA

Jodi was introduced to rug hooking by a friend 15 years ago. She started out hooking primitive rugs (with #7- to 9-cut wool) and now is using #3- to 4-cut as well. Workshops are among her favorite things; they allow her to relax from her job as a nurse. She is always inspired by other people's rugs and lives, and tries to take away one new thing from each workshop: anything from the history of rug hooking to different styles.

Adaptation of Christian, 30″ x 23″, #3- and 4-cut wool on linen. Adapted with permission from a photo by James Cattlett and hooked by Jodi Isom, Lincoln, Nebraska, 2014. JAMES CATTLETT

In the Judges' Eyes

- A unique monochromatic rug with a surprising bright touch, interesting contrasts, and a dramatic mixing of neutrals with bold color.

Ahmie

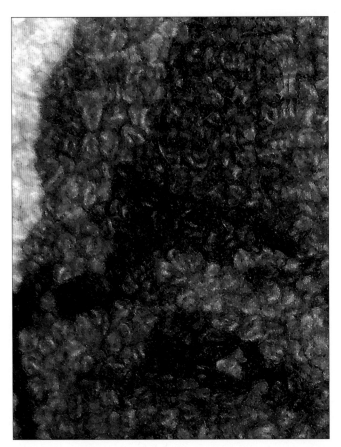

Dorr white wool, then floated the same color dye onto white wool for the mottled edging. She hooks with a #2-cut, she said, "to obtain the maximum amount of detail. I love fine shading."

While she can't put a measurement on the time from concept to finish ("A year? Six months?"), the actual hooking took about three days. "This piece came out so naturally. It was as if it happened and I just witnessed it."

Mariah has been hooking rugs "all my life, it seems"— but only five years or so seriously. "If something is worth doing it shouldn't come easily or quickly, and each piece I create demands time and quite a bit of work. But I am never sorry or feel as though I wasted my time at the end. Every piece has been worth the effort I put into it."

Favorite element of this piece? "I couldn't pick a favorite part of it. It's my grandmother's face! I love the whole thing. I love her expression."

And things learned? "I learn so much about my grandmother from everyone who sees it and shares their memories of her with me. I am still learning so much about her and welcome any and all memories... she was quite a character."

"**N**ot having the opportunity to dye, design, and hook with my grandmother is one of my biggest regrets. I wanted to feel connected to her and I wanted to pay homage to her memory and acknowledge how fortunate I am to have had so many opportunities because of her hard work."

Mariah Krauss is a fifth-generation rug hooker, "so hooking was inevitable for me! My family has owned and run Green Mountain Rug School for over 30 years and my mother started Green Mountain Hooked Rugs when I was 11 years old. I grew up in wool dust and dye pots, and was deeply connected to many of the ladies in the rug hooking world from a very young age. I've known and loved so many people in this world, including Patsy Becker, Nancy Blood, Karen Schellinger, Phyllis DeFelice, and of course my grandmother, Anne Ashworth, whom my family called Ahmie instead of Grandma."

Like all of Mariah's work, this portrait began with a paper copy of her own design and wool hand dyed specifically for the project. She created a swatch of 16 values of black on

In the Judges' Eyes

- *Skillful technical hooking and use of subtle color, outstanding values, capturing dimension with just one color in a little gem.*

MARIAH KRAUSS
MONTPELIER, VERMONT

Mariah teaches high school physical and life science and is engaged in her family's rug hooking businesses. She serves on the board of directors of the Green Mountain Rug School, is a member of the Green Mountain Rug Hooking Guild, and will be a first-time teacher at Sauder Village this year. Her work Aries Woman received Viewer's Choice and Museum Choice awards at Hooked in the Mountains in Shelburne, Vermont in 2011, as well as a Readers' Choice Award in Celebration XXII.

Ahmie, 10^1/$_2$" x 13", #2-cut hand-dyed wool on monk's cloth. Adapted with permission from a photo by Anne Knott and hooked by Mariah Krauss, Montpelier, Vermont, 2014.

Bathing Beauties

The wide range of design elements in this rug made Diane Mate "really look at skin tones, shadows, proportions, complimenting colors, contours, flow, and design. This rug is adapted from a 1920s snapshot of my mother and aunt when they were teenagers. The original black and white photo is 2¼" x 4" and has some blank spots and damage."

Diane wanted to recreate the picture in color, so she researched swimsuits of the era to create a vintage look; she also added stripes to her mother's swimsuit to add interest. "This rug was started in 2012 at the Green Lake Rug Camp with Tish Murphy. She is a face expert, so was the perfect teacher for someone who had never hooked a face. She helped draw the figures and got me started." Then the rug was set aside for a couple of years until Diane had more time to devote to hooking.

In the Judges' Eyes

- *Vibrant, whimsical use of color, facial expressions, and directional hooking in the sky and water bring this piece to life and tell the story.*

"Beside the faces, I had never hooked sand, water, or a realistic sky. The sand in the original photo was very rocky, wet, and silty looking, and I tried to capture that lumpy effect. I searched out photos of Lake Michigan and the many ways water could be hooked. I decided to hook the lake very horizontally to mimic the rolling waves. Then I determined a horizon and the change from water to the sky. Since it appeared to be a windy day, I took many pictures of clouds while walking my dog, and incorporated some of them in the rug."

Most of the wool in the rug is recycled as-is, but Diane did purchase flesh-tone wools and some supplemental dyed pieces; she also used boucle yarn and fleece to create the foam on the breaking waves. "I do not dye wool but have used onion skins and pennies, and I've marbleized and married colors." She opted for a plain dark border to keep the 1920s feel and added an Art Deco-style "bit of color" and antique white buttons in two corners. The edge is rolled forward and crocheted.

The rug holds many memories of Diane's childhood: "My siblings and I loved to tease my mother about her 'triangular' hairdo in the photo." The knee socks and beach shoes were fun to hook, and the entire rug was "definitely" a learning experience. "When I began the rug I didn't consider how much skin I would have to hook!"

DIANE ALTERGOTT MATE
ARLINGTON HEIGHTS, ILLINOIS

Diane's love of fiber arts began at the age of five with embroidery then expanded to crocheting, sewing, knitting, braiding, macramé, twining, spinning, and weaving. She discovered her love of rug hooking by means of a kit purchased at the 1999 Michigan Fiber Festival. Diane is a reenactor of the 1830s and includes rug hooking as part of her demonstration and persona. She is a demonstrator, teacher, and designer, and seeks to hone her skills and raise awareness of the craft.

Bathing Beauties, 18½" x 30½", #4- to 8-cut wool strips, yarn, and fleece, and antique buttons on linen.
Adapted from a circa 1920 family photo and hooked by Diane Altergott Mate, Arlington Heights, Illinois, 2014. CARL HERTZ

Cuba Bound

of their travels!" The photo captures the travelers in an impromptu moment, finished with their picnic lunch and enjoying some ukulele music. "By the end of the trip, all of them had learned to play."

The rug incorporates both new and recycled wool. "For the grass, I used a mix of pieces that I purchased from Marita Friedman. Her colors and the mix of overdyed tweeds and plaids made this part of the rug fun and easy to do."

The work took about a year to finish. "Most challenging were the faces and hair. The faces are about the size of a quarter, so there is not much room for shading and variation in hair color. Some of the first hair attempts were not very flattering! But, thankfully, I could take out what I didn't like and try another option."

What she learned? "That I can hook faces! The first face [far left] came together very easily. It gave me confidence to keep going." Also, "it's OK not to replicate. Working on my first pictorial in 1998, I was very reliant on the source picture and followed it as closely as I could. With each rug, I feel I've gained some confidence to make the rugs my own. The real car in *Cuba Bound* was a tomato red, and the trip was taken in early summer. I preferred the darker red for the car, and I liked the idea of an autumn trip, so I could use a variety of colors for the trees."

Anne's mom got to see the finished rug, "and I'll always remember her surprise and her fond memories of the trip. Sadly, she passed away before she learned of the *Celebration* acceptance. I'm so grateful that she introduced me to rug hooking and that we share this bond."

Anne Reeves's mother, Bernice Howell, inspired Anne to start rug hooking. She bought Anne a kit and said she thought her daughter would enjoy it. "Well, she was right."

Cuba Bound developed after Bernice's teacher, Roslyn Logsdon, suggested going through old photos for design inspiration. "This picture is of my mom and her friends, all teachers, at the end of the school year, on their trip from Minnesota to Cuba in the early 1950s. I love their spirit of adventure—six women in an old oil-guzzling car with bald tires, no door locks or working windshield wipers. They successfully made it to Cuba and back with great memories

ANNE REEVES
MONTEREY, CALIFORNIA

Anne, a public health nurse, has hooked 14 rugs, with more in progress. She credits hooking with teaching her to look at colors of objects with a finer eye: noticing the shades of green in a tree, seeing all the blues in the ocean, then thinking, "Oh, I've got the perfect piece of wool for that." Cuba Bound joins three other of her rugs that have been included in Celebration.

Cuba Bound, 19½" x 14½", #3- and 4-cut used and new wool on monk's cloth. Adapted with permission from a photo by Bernice Howell and hooked by Anne Reeves, Monterey, California, 2014. JOHN HOWELL

In the Judges' Eyes

- *Beautiful piece, with figures rendered in great detail, nice trees, and contrast with sky creating a feeling of "I want to know the story."*

Dressing on the Side: Waiter's Lament

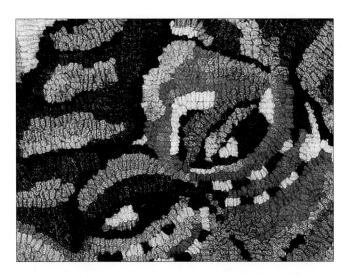

When she travels, Patricia Levin likes to collect art cards, and when she found "Fabulous Faces: Women of Colors," by Janet Mishner, "I fell in love with them. They were fun, colorful, and very different."

The rug's title comes from the caption on the original card: A busy waiter explains that he has his hands full with a regular customer, who "always wants dressing on the side," and her similarly "picky" friends: specifying toast "dry and not burnt" and nonfat milk for their coffee. "I realized I loved the subject because it reminded me of my girlfriends and our social lives together dining out—and especially our interactions with waiters."

PATRICIA ANN LEVIN
LANCASTER, PENNSYLVANIA

Pat's first class was in Lancaster, Pennsylvania, in 2007, with Peggy Hannum and Leslie Gorbey, but she'd been collecting articles about rug hooking since 1970. She loves exploring different materials and techniques and takes as many classes as she can. "I would say I am developing my style at the same time that I am discovering my style," and her favorite teachers are textile artists in all media who support her personal exploration.

The dyed wool in the piece came mostly from Peggy Hannum. "I used hand-dyed wool yarn of various types for areas of the hair and faces, to provide texture and work into small spaces." The needle-felted title on the tablecloth is hand-dyed roving. Pat wanted to use the script style of the original art for both the title and the plate monograms, "and the needle felting allowed me to do that easily." She chose the letter "J" as the monogram to evoke "both Janet's name and my maiden name of Justice."

A particular challenge was trying to use Peggy's spot-dyed wool in the background so that it looked like paint strokes. Pat finally cut the wool into various widths and hooked vertically. She remembered advice from Roslyn Lodgsdon "that it is sometimes difficult, if not impossible" to make hooking look like painting, so Pat started focusing on "hooking what I saw and not what I wanted to make it look like—which helped a great deal but was still a struggle." Pat used as-is black and white herringbone wool for the tablecloth.

The colors are those used by the artist in the original card, but Pat expanded on the original painting to include dinner plates, a tablecloth, and parts of menus and hands that were not in the original frame. "I love how the faces, with all the different colors and textures, reflect the different personalities of the three gals and express their attitudes at that moment when their friend asks for her dressing on the side. I also like the way the viewer is drawn into the rug and has to explore what is happening."

One of the things she learned from the rug: "Patience! I had to hook different areas of the rug in many different ways to achieve what I wanted to achieve, and that meant working and reworking and using the information from many different teachers and reading resources."

In the Judges' Eyes

- *Bold graphics, colors full of impact and life, set off by black and white plaid, offering lots to wonder at and study.*

Dressing on the Side: Waiter's Lament, 38" x 28", #3- to 7-cut hand-dyed and as-is wool, wool yarn, and needle-felted wool roving on linen. Adapted with permission from art work by Janet Mishner and hooked by Patricia Ann Levin, Lancaster, Pennsylvania, 2014. IMPACT XPOZURES

End of the Day

Janice Lee wanted to adapt a photograph of her son, Will Arington, taken by his friend Heather DePra, right after he finished working cattle. "The picture shows the tired cowboy, holding a beer he had just been handed, resting against the cattle-working chute. The shadow of his tired horse is silhouetted beside him. You can just pick up the shape of the horse's ear and lowered head. The picture was a masterpiece, from the tired man and horse to the sueded knees on his worn jeans. Even the buckles on his spurs were significant to me."

She hooked most of the rug "in a whirlwind three days" during a Diane Stoffel class, and finished it completely in the next two weeks.

"One of the funny moments of this class was when all the ladies got in on the deliberation of the brand of beer on the can. I insisted my son is a Busch Light drinker, but someone else thought it looked like a Bud Light. Leave it to a doctor in the group to look up the artwork online. It was indeed a Bud Light. When I asked my son about it he said, 'You know, mom, at *the end of the day*, you drink whatever brand of beer somebody hands you.' I knew I had my title. I had been saying to people that it just looks like 'the end of the day.' Now Will confirmed it.

"Because I own a store and dye my own wool, there was no problem coming up with the various shades of blue for the project. Almost everything, except the hat, shirt, boots, and dirt, is a different shade and texture of blue."

The dirt gave her the most trouble. "I redid the dirt three

times before I was satisfied. I tried to get too fancy with the ground, adding too much detail. Finally, I made it more subtle and boring, just like dirt should be, and was much happier with the result."

When her son saw the finished results, he jokingly called it "shoddy workmanship," Janice wrote. "He said, 'I had on a plaid shirt that day and I have never worn a hat quite that shade of tan. Nope, shoddy workmanship is all I can say.'"

The rug is now her favorite. "It shows my real-life son, in his real-life job. And the stories I can tell about this rug also show how irritating he can be as his real-life self. And I wouldn't have him any other way."

JANICE LEE
VALLEY, NEBRASKA

Janice considers herself a primitive rug hooker; she started with a primitive teacher in 2001. In her journey, she studied with Pris Buttler and Diane Stoffel, and credits them with teaching her "how fulfilling (and challenging) rug hooking can be." The owner of The Rug Hooking Store at Black Horse Antiques, Janice's Ghost Horse was a finalist in Celebration XXIII. The Vestal Virgins rugs from a Master Class at her store were featured in the November 2014 issue of Rug Hooking *magazine.*

In the Judges' Eyes

- *Perfect rustic frame, with colors and contrast offering the right feel for a hot day, and fabulous directional hooking and muted colors.*

End of the Day, 22" x 33", #4- and 6-cut wool on linen. Adapted with permission from a photo by Heather DePra and hooked by Janice Lee, Valley, Nebraska, 2014. SCOTT AVERY

Floral Triptych

The celebrated floral photography of David Leaser was the inspiration for this work, by Kerri Kolbe, and she was particularly attracted to the composition of each piece. David Leaser is known for his detailed photos of individual flowers against plain black or white backgrounds—using the same technology, his website notes, that NASA used to capture images on Mars. His work has been cited in *Architectural Digest* and *Nikon World*, and honored with a Silver Medal at the International Photography Awards, a "Best in the West" designation by *Sunset* magazine, and, in 2014, earned First Place in the Flower category and Grand Champion in the Nature category at the Moscow International Foto Awards.

With such detailed realism as inspiration, Kerri's goal was to create images that were as realistic and dimensional as possible. She also identified different concepts in each section: "The Night Flower was about depth and movement, the Dahlia about distinguishing redundant petals, and the

Parrot Tulip about form." While the three flowers in this triptych function as a unit, Kerri sees them as a theme with lots of potential for variation.

"I wanted the three panels to be able to stand alone yet work together. Changing the 'order' of how the flowers are displayed can change the feel of the piece. The triptych is displayed in a stairwell with a ceiling height of over 12 feet. They can be displayed horizontally or stacked vertically."

While most of the piece is hooked with wool, "each section has different components, unified by the common 'neutral' black wool background. The Night Flower (green) has a composite material for the yellow stamens so they project out from the center. The Dahlia has silk petals that surround the center, and each petal is outlined with triple embroidery threads."

The three-part work took Kerri about a year to complete, and "I'm a relatively new rug hooker, so I am still challenged by techniques like shading. I'm fortunate to

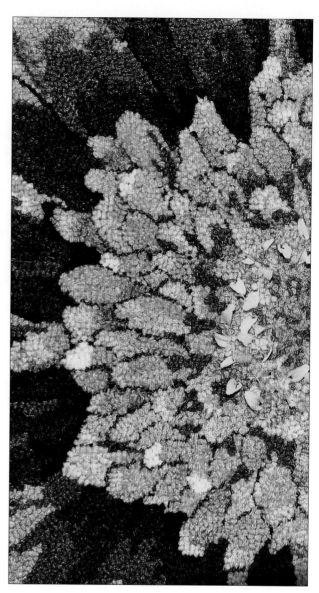

have a great teacher, Judy Fresk, who can offer suggestions and guidance."

Each section has been stretched taut over a wooden board, with the linen stapled to the back.

"My favorite part was creating the varying forms that each flower required to make it appear as they exist in nature, three-dimensional rather than flat. This was also my greatest challenge." The use of additional materials helped to create the look she sought.

Floral Triptych, three panels 22" x 23" each, #3-cut wool, embroidery thread, and composite materials on linen. Adapted with permission from photos by David Leaser and hooked by Kerri Kolbe, Bolton, Connecticut, 2014.

In the Judges' Eyes

- *Simplicity of composition, with bold use of complex and complementary colors; well executed forms that "pop" against the very dark background.*

KERRI KOLBE
BOLTON, CONNECTICUT

Kerri began rug hooking classes with Judy Fresk in 2011 after seeing an article about Judy in the local newspaper. She hooked four rugs her first year. Now retired from a career in corporate financial management, she is interested in creating images and forms using colors and textures. This is the second appearance of her work in Celebration.

Girl with a BIG Bow

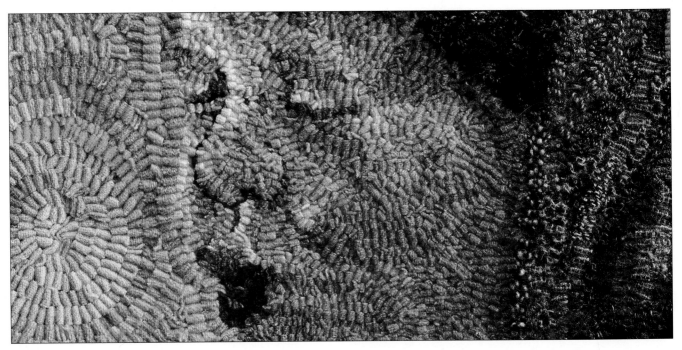

T his piece came about in a class taught by Tish Murphy, "who is known for her portraits." Sharon McKendry loves children, and she was "caught by the photo (by photographer Alison Beachem in the online children's magazine, *Babiekins)* because of the girl's outrageous bow. Her sweet face and profile were wonderful. A bit of whimsy and a fun expression."

The piece took four to five months to complete. "The most challenging part of portraits for me is usually the eyes and the nose." Also, "in my portrait classes with Tish Murphy, I've learned that adding those unexpected little colors can be exciting—like a dash of purple on a face." Her favorite part of the image is the girl's lips: "They are so luscious."

Sharon has only done "a tiny bit" of wool dyeing; she gets most of her wool from Paulette Wentzlaff, at River Rock Wool in Hudson, Wisconsin. "Her colors are vibrant and lovely."

When considering how to finish the rug, "I love scallops so I decided to stuff them with rice and have the weight help hold the piece in place. Black and white stripes are something that I use a lot, so I finished the back with a graphic look.

"I've never made a *rug.* After finishing my first piece (a chicken), I found a man to make an ottoman to fit the chicken pattern. Then, with the help of a talented upholstery woman, we designed the ottoman with piping and a ruffled edge. I can't seem to want to walk on my pieces. One of my pieces was turned into a thick bench seat cushion, so my son built me a chest to fit it, and it sits at the end of my bed. Again, I added piping and a ruffle. I love embellishment and whimsy! I had fun painting the bench with some of the same motifs as the cushion. I like to ask myself what else I can do with a piece to push its

SHARON MCKENDRY
CRYSTAL, MINNESOTA

After resisting rug hooking because it was "one more thing with more supplies," Sharon went to a festival on Mother's Day some five years ago and a chicken pattern caught her eye. She took her first lesson from Victoria Jacobson at Angel-Girl Rug Hooking Studio. With a background in teaching art to children, advertising, and photography, Sharon's passion is color. She is working on a color and design class for fiber artists, and continues to knit, crochet, quilt, sew, make glass beads and jewelry, punchneedle, embroider, and felt.

Girl with a BIG Bow, 20″ circle, #3- and 8-cut wool on monk's cloth, with rice-filled fabric scallops, and fabric piping and backing. Adapted with permission from a photo by Alison Beachem and hooked by Sharon McKendry, Crystal, Minnesota, 2014. TOM THULEN

boundaries; thus, I made *Girl with a BIG Bow* as a cover for my floor frame."

In thinking about this piece, Sharon "discovered that I 'love' a lot of things; color, design, composition, photography, embellishment, whimsy, and children. I love rug hooking because of the strong community of loving, hardworking women."

In the Judges' Eyes

- *A fun, original, cheery interpretation with great choice of colors; the round theme plays out in the stuffed border.*

Journey 1941–2004

Sheila Mitchell's parents "were not much for telling family stories." But, in 2007, "my mother was encouraged to take part in writing her personal experiences as a War Bride coming to Canada for a museum project in Medicine Hat, Alberta. This was the basis for my story rug—her and my father's story from the time they met to the time my father passed away."

When Sheila began the actual work, "I realized quickly it was not so easy to put together such a personal story." First, the rug was to be a teaching piece for border design at a McGown Teachers Workshop. "I retained the size of the border but removed much of the complexity, leaving only the lines dividing the spaces." Also, the "window" of the panel presented a restricted size of 13³/4" x 25", limiting opportunities for creativity. Finally, "photographs tell a lot

about a family, but it is so hard to interpret what the lives of those were like without the stories that go with the photos."

Sheila used mostly new and some recycled wool from her stash. The show binding is an acrylic tartan fabric from a pleated skirt, chosen for its colors." After first attaching it alone as the show binding and feeling unhappy with the effect, I removed it and sewed in strips of quilt batting to puff it up, giving it more balance with the hooked work."

The only dyeing she did was the border. "The khaki color is to represent my father being in the Canadian Army and going to England to train for war." She also included some of the khaki in the rest of the rug as an integrating element. The train was perhaps the more challenging element, "but also a fun part, and so really kept me focused. I am pleased with the result. Perhaps the portrait was the most difficult to hook, as the space is small and I was working from an old black and white photograph."

Sheila "put pencil to paper for the actual drawing" on March 30, 2014, and finished hooking it on June 20, 2014.

"*Journey* is significant to me on a personal level as I designed and hooked it after my mother's passing. In a way it was a 'grieving piece' for me, but it brought me a 'healing peace,' too, as it forced me to think on many happy memories. The rug had almost a voice of its own, 'telling' me to include flowers." The idea had not previously occurred to her, "but my mom always loved flowers, so I made them a part of the story and the journey."

In the Judges' Eyes

- A wonderful old-world feel with lots of story in a beautiful palette, with the border offering a pleasing contrast to the well-flowing center.

SHEILA MITCHELL
VICTORIA, BRITISH COLUMBIA, CANADA

A McGown Certified Instructor, Sheila creates designs for her own rugs and to assist students; she also dyes her own wool, primarily for her workshops. Although she does not specialty dye for students, she does like to prepare backgrounds for them to explore new techniques. Hooking bird images has been a focus for several years. Sheila serves on the board for TIGHR (The International Guild of Handhooking Rugmakers) and is very busy this year preparing for the Triennial in Victoria, British Columbia, in October.

Journey 1941–2004, 23¹/₂″ x 34″, #3-,4- and 5-cut hand-dyed, new, and recycled wool on linen, with tartan fabric padded border. Adapted from family photos and hooked by Sheila Mitchell, Victoria, British Columbia, Canada, 2014. JOHN MITCHELL

Kai's Jack

Kathleen Harwood's oldest grandson, Kai, "has been intrigued by cards since he was small and now, at 15, he is an accomplished magician. When I decided that I would, over time, make a rug for each of my grandsons, it was easy to know where to start." She "casually" asked Kai if he had a favorite card, and—yes, the Jack of Diamonds.

Kathleen wanted to retain the limited palette of the traditional card "but, with so few colors, they had to be brilliant and perfect. Jan Cole, of The Wool'n Gardener, dyed me the lush red and wonderful yellows that I requested. The rich, deep blue, chosen because I felt the black of the card would be too harsh, is Nancy Jewett's (Fluff & Peachy Bean Designs) Liberty Blue; I kept going back to her for more, as the rug seemed to devour it." Glittery threads were woven into some of the red and as-is cream areas.

"I feared it might be boring to hook, since it's a rigid composition of mirror images in limited colors. But I love surface pattern, and I enjoyed every minute. It's such a baroque, rich surface, and there was so much challenging variation to get right that there wasn't time to get bored."

Challenges? "I avoided those faces as long as I could. I don't hook people, never had the slightest interest. Thought it would be impossible to get these Jacks' visages right. But they do play a pretty significant part in the rug and finally I couldn't work around them anymore. And guess what? They were no trouble at all. They flowed right off my hook. I liked them when they were done and kicked myself for all that angst."

The rug was finished by rolling the backing to the front and crocheting with two strands of wool, one deep blue and one black, to blend with the rug border. Lessons learned: "I did not need to learn this, but I was reminded how satisfying it is to make something for someone you love. I was also reminded how important it is to work with just the right materials. I learned that those folks who designed the traditional playing cards centuries ago really knew what they were doing. And I did actually think of an easy way to make one end of the rug a mirror image of the other using simple technology: I took a picture of the completed half and blew up details of it on my iPad, which I kept next to me for comparison while hooking the second one. This was especially helpful with the second face; I could actually count the loops."

KATHLEEN HARWOOD
SOUTH HADLEY, MASSACHUSETTS

Kathleen Harwood is an art historian and a fine art consultant and appraiser; she appears regularly as an appraiser of paintings on PBS's Antiques Roadshow. She learned to hook in 2002 "at the knees of Nancy McClelland and Claire de Roos and they remain mentors and friends; how lucky am I?" She simply loves to hook and "I know it is one of the important things that keeps me sane and centered. It's kind of like stationary yoga."

In the Judges' Eyes

- An exhilarating rug for card-lovers, with beautiful, crisp color and line, effective use of beading, and blue dyed wool that does something magic to the whole piece.

Kai's Jack, 30" x 55", #4-, 6- and 8-cut wool on linen. Adapted from a traditional playing card and hooked by Kathleen Harwood, South Hadley, Massachusetts, 2014.

VAN ZANDBERGEN PHOTOGRAPHY

Lucy

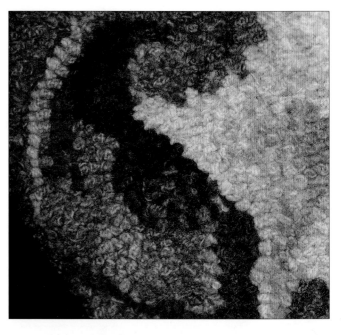

Mary McGrath believes that rug hookers "have all been blessed with a talent: a talent we are tasked with sharing with others. I have several really close girlfriends, and I decided to hook a rug for each of them. Lucy was a special horse that my friend Shawn owned. Shawn unfortunately lost Lucy to health complications in the fall of 2012."

Leonard Feenan created the pattern from a photo of Lucy, and Mary hooked the rug with hand-dyed swatches from Carol Kassera.

"The most challenging parts of this rug were her eyes. Mary started with the full eye. "The photograph shows a very dark eye that had little variation to it, so getting a realistic, believable eye was difficult." Her instructor, Carol Kassera, "walked me through" that challenge. "Then, when I had to hook her left eye, I reverse hooked that several times because I couldn't get the shape just right."

Another great challenge was eliminating, at Shawn's request, the halter that had obscured parts of Lucy's face in the original photo. "I felt at times like I was hooking her blindly," so Mary found online reference images that could help her recreate the missing areas.

Her favorite aspect of the rug: "I personally love how the muscles translated onto the wool. Lucy was a large Holsteiner mare who had a thick neck and a beautifully muscled chest and shoulder area. Actually everything about

her was large, and when I stand back and look at the rug, I see her as she was in life."

She started hooking *Lucy* in September 2013 and completed the rug in October 2014.

Lessons taught by this rug? "By hooking this piece I actually grew stronger in my faith—I know that may seem like an odd statement, but I think for me that was the simplest message. When I was hooking and got stuck in a difficult place and it wasn't hooking the way my eye was seeing it in the photograph, I would ask God for help and to guide me. This happened many, many times, and each time I found my way past the challenge and the result was beautiful. I have often told others that I was merely the instrument—because I asked for divine intervention so often, and the end result is more than I could have ever imagined."

The rug now hangs in Shawn's home, "and she has told me that looking at it brings her internal calmness."

MARY MCGRATH
MUKWONAGO, WISCONSIN

Mary started rug hooking in 2003 after seeing a primitive hand-hooked rug at a quilt shop. "The idea wouldn't let go." Her "wonderfully well-rounded teacher, Joyce Krueger" has "gently encouraged" her growth. As a working mother of young children, Mary currently purchases dyed wools for her work, "though mastering the art of dyeing is definitely on my bucket list." A member of ATHA (Association of Traditional Hooking Artists), she tries to hook each evening: "The rug seems to absorb me as the problems, worries, and issues from the day evaporate." This is the third of Mary's rugs that have appeared in Celebration.

In the Judges' Eyes

- *Good use of value shading to create three-dimensionality, obvious hooking skills, great background choice and beautiful contrast with horse; love the detail in the nose.*

Lucy, *18"x 24", #3-cut wool on rug warp. Adapted, with permission, by Leonard Feenan, from a photograph by Shawn Minnich, and hooked by Mary McGrath, Mukwonago, Wisconsin, 2014.* ART'S CAMERAS PLUS

Mary Rose

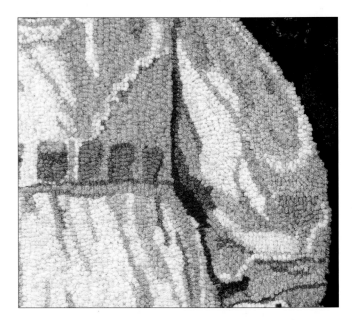

Marilyn Becker chose the design for *Mary Rose* from a family photo of her mother, Mary Rose Gresl-Janke-Johnas. "I loved the dress she wore and wondered if I could duplicate it in a rug. I knew it would be a challenge."

She also wanted to learn more about hooking faces. Marilyn loved the folds and tucks in the dress fabric, and the daisies along the lower edge of the skirt—which took about two months to complete.

The technique she used, after trial and error, was to take a piece of #2-cut white wool about 8 inches long, twist it loosely around the rug hook, gently hook the loose end of the wool and pull it through the "tunnel" of wool, then pull it tighter "until it looks like a cocoon with wool sticking out of both ends. That's *one* daisy petal." Then she hooked the wool ends into place through the backing. Each daisy required 10 petals. For the centers, Marilyn made pom-poms, cut them Waldoboro style, and sewed them into place with heavy quilting thread. She pulled loops of pink and beige between the daisy petals "and the flower was done." Finally, she sewed all of the petals onto the backing with heavy quilting thread.

"Another thing I wanted to do with this rug was make it from *all* naturally dyed wool fabric. My sister gave me a bushel of walnuts, and I dyed yards and yards of natural Dorr wool." She achieved various shades of walnut, but not the dark chocolate she wanted for the background. "So when I saw dark chocolate wool on a bolt, I use that for

most of the background. Also, the white-white on the dress is as-is, off the bolt fabric. The rest I dyed with rose petals, beets, blackberries, leaves, nuts, tea, etc." The chair was mostly done with the walnut-dyed wool. "Oh, her shoes were from a black skirt my Mom had years ago that she gave to me."

In addition to the daisies, the most challenging part of the rug was the face "which I did over about 10 times. Now I love her."

Marilyn finished the rug by hand-sewing half-inch gold silky upholstery braid along the edge, then sewing strips of heavy coating fabric, zig-zagged on both edges, to the braid, and tacking it to the rug with loose stitches.

"What did I learn from the rug? I guess I learned that I can do faces to my satisfaction, if I keep correcting them and do not give up. If I hadn't corrected this face, I would never have liked the rug, and it would have been wasted time for me."

MARILYN BECKER
WAUSAU, WISCONSIN

Marilyn credits her mother, "a hard-working farm wife" with an artistic flair, for her interest in art and textiles. Marilyn and her sisters made their own clothing, including wedding gowns; Marilyn took French hand-sewing lessons to make dresses for her granddaughters and was an avid quilter. She started hooking in 1996 then, *dissatisfied with the results, put it away until 2012. Now "it is my obsession." Her rug* Marry Me, Mary *was a finalist in Celebration XXIV.*

In the Judges' Eyes

- *Great portrait work in a selective palette, lovely skin tones with contrast making for a huge impact in quiet subject matter; masterful lace work shows great technical hooking skills; detail on the chair and dress are amazing.*

Mary Rose, 32¹/₂″ x 58″, #3- and 4-cut natural-dyed and off-the-bolt wool on cotton rug warp. Adapted from a family photo and hooked by Marilyn Becker, Wausau, Wisconsin, 2014. GALL PHOTO

Michel—Marcilly sur Eure

After getting Monique's permission to adapt the photo, Carol began adding to the composition. "There was a huge black space on the left of the photo. Only the right window and curtain were showing. I added the window on the left side of the hooking, a potted geranium on the window sill, and suggested something going on in the interior."

Next was the color choice. "Even though this was a black and white photo, the colors seemed to be so obvious. What other color would a French shutter be, but a faded blue? The curtains had to be a sun faded red and white check with a sheer on top. The little boy's bike probably wasn't red, but it seemed perfect for the composition. All that was left to do was to have fun hooking."

The only wool that had to be dyed for this piece was the greenish blue for the shutter. All fabrics were wools recycled from thrift shops, except the dark gray wool that Carol bought for the interior of the home. "I had every shade of gray except the one needed, saw it, and was too lazy to dye another piece."

Carol's favorite part of the rug is, "of course, all the texture. The shutter was the whole reason I chose this design. It really thrilled me to depict the worn peeling paint on the shutter using only shades of color. I also enjoyed doing the same for the mottled wall and concrete window sill."

The biggest challenge was hooking the curtains. "There was no problem with using a gray for the shadow in the gathers of the fabric, but how to do the checks? I decided to make rounded stripes of dull pink. The rounding of the stripes show the curve of the gathers in the hanging curtain. The stripes also suggest the check without having to hook little tiny squares. At the top, a paler pink and gray are used to suggest that the checked curtains show through the sheers."

This hooking now hangs in Monique's home. When she first saw it completed, she said it brought her "right back to where she grew up."

Carol Koerner fell in love with a small black and white snapshot that her friend, Monique Hafrey, took when she was a teenager in France around 1940. "I couldn't get it out of my mind. The texture of the worn paint on the shutter, and the old mottled wall called out to me. Hooking different textures is my thing, and I couldn't wait to hook these."

The little boy in the photo was Monique's little cousin, Michel, who died at a young age many years ago.

CAROL KOERNER
BETHESDA, MARYLAND

This is the eleventh time that Carol's work has appeared in an edition of Celebration. *Three of her pieces have won Readers' Choice recognition, and 10 other pieces have appeared in* The ATHA Newsletter, *three of them on the cover. She has written two articles for* Rug Hooking *magazine: "Hooked Matryoshka Dolls" (June/July/Aug 2007), and "The Art of the Series: A Sweet Suite" (March/April/May 2012).*

In the Judges' Eyes

- *Unique subject matter with a very French "feel," supported by effective use of light colors and the "pop" of red bicycle and flowers to add interest; love the curtains.*

Michel—Marcilly sur Eure, 23″ x 30″, #3-cut wool on linen. Adapted with permission from a photograph by Monique Hafrey and hooked by Carol Koerner, Bethesda, Maryland, 2014.

Peacock

More than three decades ago, a friend introduced Elissa Crouch to rug hooking. "Here I am, 35 years later, doing what I love to do. I hook almost every day. It is my creative outlet."

Each step in the process of creating a rug "is like a different profession: drawing, dyeing and then the actual hooking. It is magical to watch a pattern come to life. You plan and plan, and nothing prepares you for the 'pop' that happens, when you know it is right."

Inspiration for her designs "come from everywhere," Elissa wrote. "I am surrounded by artists, and we charge our batteries from talking to each other. My family are all artists (mostly painters; one woodworker). My artistic vision has been influenced by my friends and this path through life. You never know where it might come from, and it is always exciting when it slams you in the back."

Peacock was a collaborative process that came from a conversation with friend and jewelry artist and designer Joyce Fritz Ritz. "After telling her about my rug hooking friends doing peacocks, she went right to work drawing one (influenced by a Zentangle™ class we had taken). When she showed it to me, I knew that it was a design I had to hook."

Together, they collaborated on a show of jewelry in peacock colors and other pieces of Joyce's art interpreted in hooking; the pieces formed a show at a local gallery.

"The peacock was made from leftovers from other projects and as-is wool (black watch plaid). I only dyed for the background." This rug is now in a private collection.

"My favorite part of the rug is the face. If you get the 'life' in the eyes, for me, it then becomes my pet and it is easy to finish him. It took almost a month of constant hooking to complete."

The challenging part was getting the design as close as possible to the original art, Elissa wrote. "If I questioned where it was going, I would call Joyce. She would stop in and we would banter the problem about and then come up with the solution."

The rug was bound with wool strips to match the background, rolling the linen to the back.

"I would encourage everyone to do a collaboration with an artist whose work you admire and respect. It is one of the most treasured experiences to share your art with another who reciprocates exactly how you feel."

ELISSA CROUCH
CAMBRIDGE, MARYLAND

Elissa worked alone for years, and then found a local group headed by Mary Sheppard Burton. After earning her McGown certification, she taught evening classes at The Chesapeake College, and recently taught at a senior center. She attends rug camps and schools as often as possible. "I never stop learning." She dyes most of her wool and creates original patterns. Her work is sold in local galleries. This is the second appearance of her work in Celebration.

In the Judges' Eyes

- *Love the composition and the use of a repeated scroll design in the background, must have huge impact in person: the touch of warm color with cool blues and purples is very well done.*

Peacock, 52" x 72", #3- to 6-cut wool on linen. Adapted with permission from an illustration by Joyce Fritz Ritz and hooked by Elissa Crouch, Cambridge, Maryland, 2014. DAVID HARP

Piggy

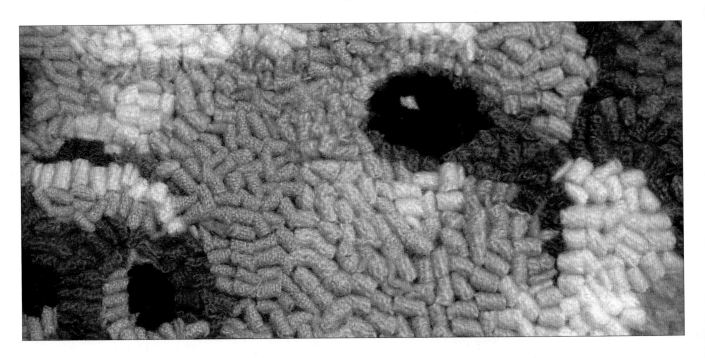

"Successful artistic endeavors don't evolve in a vacuum, and, in this case, 'It took a village!'" Kristen Brown chose this design "because I enjoy the way painters often choose unexpected colors that the viewer's eye interprets as something else. (For example, a 'white' cow may be rendered in pinks, blues, and yellows.) After visiting oil painter Craig Blietz's studio in Door County, Wisconsin, I decided to experiment with that technique in wool on a very small scale. Blietz's farm animal paintings are often room-sized."

With the permission of photographer Kathy Milani, the photographer, Kristen chose to interpret the image of a baby pig from the cover of a Humane Society magazine. "He strikes an assertive pose while being undeniably cute!"

She followed April DeConick's advice in the book, *Wool Snapshots*, and made a full-sized black and white copy of the magazine cover. "With that in hand, I could hook entirely from values and simply play with colors that suited my value requirements. The process required lots and lots of squinting as I judged value blends. I also used a reducing glass to continually evaluate how the forms as a whole were rounding out."

"I started this rug at Green Lake Rug Hooking Camp with Eric Sandburg as my teacher. As my 'experiment' took shape, he assured me that it was working. He also encouraged me to enter it for judging in *Celebration*."

The rug took about a month to complete, and the biggest challenge was to keep the entire rug to the same level of detail.

"Honestly, I was truly surprised by the three-dimensional look of this little piggy. It is gratifying to see how the influences of oil painting, animal photography, a new book, and an encouraging teacher can unite to make a piggy almost pop out of the rug."

Kristen particularly likes using repurposed wool. "In fact, a few holes or stains make it much easier to slice a finely tailored garment to smithereens!" She recently experienced

KRISTEN BROWN
CHIPPEWA FALLS, WISCONSIN

Five years ago, as she was becoming an empty-nester, an evening community education class popped up: "Wool Rug Hooking." Within three months, Kristen had a frame, a good cutter, and a subscription to Rug Hooking magazine. She has completed 21 rugs, 20 of them original designs. Piggy is her first adaptation.

Piggy, 18″ x 18″, #5- and 6-cut overdyed and hand-dyed new and repurposed wool on linen. Adapted with permission from a photo by Kathy Milani and hooked by Kristen Brown, Chippewa Falls, Wisconsin, 2014. JEFFREY BROWN

"repurposed fabric" at a new level while hooking alongside rural Mayan women in the western highlands of Guatemala.

"Wool is not available to them, so we all bravely plunged into piles of thrift store cast-offs and hooked with everything from t-shirts to baby sleepers. The innate artistic sense of the Mayan women is inspiring."

Teacher and rug-hooker Mary Anne Wise has worked for five years to establish this rug-hooking cooperative and to develop a new market niche to help impoverished women. Her time in Guatemala reminded Kristen that "most of us in the rug-hooking world regard hooking as somewhere on the continuum between pastime and passion. The Mayans acknowledge that it may keep them from hunger or homelessness. That is a contrast worth pondering."

In the Judges' Eyes

• *A memorable piece; love the puddling of values and color, the spare and subtle use of texture and plaid. Such a sweet and friendly pig! Who knew pigs could be so pretty?*

Rip Curl

Rip Curl is adapted from the design "Rip Curl II" created by Amanda Corrigan for her family's business, Coastal Prezence. Coastal Prezence makes their original designs out of real pieces of seaweed that they arrange and photograph for their prints and cards.

Sunny Runnels "loves the outdoors—that's where I find beauty. Our house is decorated with bowls of smooth river rocks, agates, pieces of beautiful drift wood, and all things related to birds: carvings, paintings, nests, feathers, and weathered skulls. The beauty all around me is what I enjoy hooking."

What drew Sunny to this design: The fluid coil and "the visual change of the leaves as they age. The rug was a birthday gift for my daughter. She's an avid kayaker, loves the ocean, and this is her favorite type of seaweed." The rug now lives in her daughter's home, a heritage house in Victoria.

"Dip dyeing wool to show the value change in each leaf was my first thought, but then the color play began. It was a challenge and a whole lot of fun combining colors while keeping the gradual value change in each leaf as well as in the total plant."

Sunny had a "really difficult time" deciding on the background color. "I was at a hook-in with lots of talented women so I asked for everyone's ideas. The idea she chose came from a woman who said, 'The linen backing looks great with the seaweed—just do something similar.' That's why I spot dyed with just one color. I didn't want a smooth background since I thought that my daughter would use this on her kitchen floor, and a variety of values might hide some spills."

She finished the piece by rolling the backing forward and binding it with wool yarn. "It was very difficult to block into a rectangle because of all the diagonal hooking I'd done."

Sunny's first rugs were patterns, "but I quickly realized that what I enjoy is hooking pieces that are personal—memories or things I love."

Sunny holds a bachelor's degree in interior design and attends many regional workshops and rug camps. She's also traveled to dyeing class with Wanda Kerr, a hooking class with Deanne Fitzpatrick and Doris Eaton, and Hooked in the Mountains.

She considers herself a realist hooker, "but I'm learning to play with color. I love dyeing wool and have tried all sorts of dyeing methods."

SUNNY RUNNELLS
LANTZVILLE, BRITISH COLUMBIA, CANADA

A neighbor of Sunny had hooked for years, "but it wasn't until I pulled my first loop that I fell in love with the craft. The process is very simple, but the possibilities are endless." She has been hooking for 13 years. This is her third appearance in Celebration.

In the Judges' Eyes

- *Background color and value shading shows great skill, lovely and dynamic use of different but closely valued colors; love the choice of artwork.*

Rip Curl, 49″ x 30″, #6-cut wool on linen. Adapted with permission from the art print "Rip Curl 2," by Amanda Corrigan for Coastal Prezence, and hooked by Sunny Runnells, of Lantzville, British Columbia, Canada, 2014.

That's Some Good Hat, Harry!

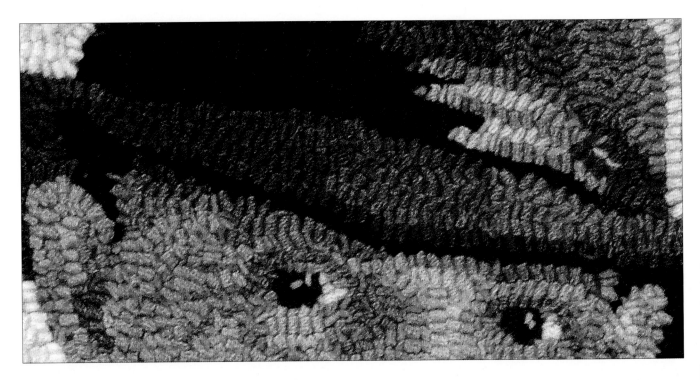

Maureen Page was looking through photos that her husband had taken and stored on the computer "when I saw this picture of my father, Harry Boothroyd. I knew I had to hook it."

The occasion had been an Easter party at Maureen's home. Her father attended wearing a hat he had just purchased. "He always wore hats because he had lupus and needed to protect himself from the sun."

Maureen adapted the original photo by removing other people and simplifying the background.

"I liked the angle of the doorway and the room behind him, the way his hat was backlit, and the front/side lighting of his left side." These were also the most challenging elements.

"I wanted to show the backlighting of his hat and the sidelighting of his arm. I also wanted to show the angles of the rooms, but with very few details. The vision was in my head, but I had no idea how it was going to turn out. I'm not sure if I would do it again."

Lesson from the rug: Hooking the jacket taught her how to create the look of fabric.

Maureen has hooked 10 rugs since she began—after retiring from work as a computer programmer. She usually dyes her own wool and designs her own patterns. She studied horticulture in college, so loves the forms of flowers and landscapes, but she is also interested in faces and the form of the human body.

In this work, "my father's eyes and his pose, with his hand in his pocket," are her favorite elements.

MAUREEN PAGE
MIDDLETOWN, CONNECTICUT

Maureen is a member of the Vermont Rug Hooking Guild and recently exhibited two rugs in their Hooked in the Mountains show. This is her second work to appear in Celebration. *Her rug* The Boy with Far Away Eyes *was a finalist in* Celebration XXIV.

That's Some Good Hat, Harry!, 24¹/₂" x 29", #3- and 4-cut 8-value swatches, spot-dyed and dip-dyed wool, and Tish Murphy's *Flesh Tone Wool Packet on monk's cloth. Adapted from a family photo and hooked by Maureen Page, Middletown, Connecticut, 2014.*

In the Judges' Eyes

- *Creative compostion with great lines, colors that express the vintage feel of the subject, demonstrating fantastic shading and value skills; Harry just comes to life here!*

The Abandoned Shack

Linda Folger's first teacher was her cousin's wife, Kay Rautenberg, certified by Jane McGown Flynn and "a marvelous teacher. She taught me not only the technique of hooking, but more importantly, how to *look* at things; for example, not just seeing a flower but each individual petal, with all the intricate shading."

Linda's preference is for "intricate commercial patterns or my own designs or adaptations, using mainly #3- and 4-cut wool."

She is a member ("though inactive") of the Western Reserve Rug Hooking Guild. "I've never sold any of my rugs, but my three children have a number of them in their homes. Kay; my husband, Tom (of 50 years); and my children have all provided inspiration and encouragement—invaluable!"

This piece is her first entry in any contest. "I am honored to have it displayed alongside works by so many truly gifted rug hookers."

The rug—actually a wall hanging—is "an adaptation of a painting by Carl Gaertner, which was given to my father-in-law, Dr. G. Keith Folger, as a gift for delivering Mr. Gaertner's children. The date of the untitled painting, which I call *The Abandoned Shack*, is 1940. Mr. Gaertner died in 1952."

The wool for the piece, a combination of old and new, came from Kay and from "the wonderful people at W. Cushing." The work took about seven months to complete.

The entire piece was, essentially, a challenge in shading, and the most challenging part was the shack itself, "with all its shading to make it look 'abandoned.' A lot of hooking,

and a lot of taking out, went into the lonely shack!"

Which turned out to be one of Linda's favorite elements, along with "the broken-down fence, the rich, earthy tones in the landscape, and the stormy sea."

The rug is finished with whipped yarn and framed. It hangs in the living room of her son's mountain home.

LINDA FOLGER
SHAKER HEIGHTS, OHIO

Linda learned to hook in 1978, but stopped hooking after a few years to work as an RN at the Cleveland Clinic. She retired in 2005 "and resumed my passion for hooking." Altogether, she has hooked 15 rugs and three small primitive pieces. This is the first time her work has appeared in Celebration.

In the Judges' Eyes

- *Takes a simple subject and gives it rich texture and a compelling story through the use of color, contrast, and perspective; keeps the viewer's eye moving and using their imagination; directional hooking very effective in this piece.*

The Abandoned Shack, 33" x 24", #2- to 4-cut wool on linen. Adapted from a painting by Carl Gaertner and hooked by Linda Folger, Shaker Heights, Ohio, 2014. BRUCE FOLGER

Thornbirds

R oland Nunn says that he does not have "natural artistic abilities" but has attended many workshops in his development as a rug hooker. He also cites the influence of his mother, Clarice, who hooked rugs in the 1950s and whose work, along with his own, is showcased on his Facebook page.

His dyeing is detailed and precise, as evidenced in his discussion of his work *Floravians* in the November/December 2014 issue of *Rug Hooking* magazine. For that piece, Roland used nine swatches from four different dye formulas, five being transitional swatches. He also used a single piece of wool for the sky. He works exclusively in #3-cut and mainly in swatches.

Roland is eclectic in his selection of images for hooking projects. "I use calendar photos and greeting cards as source material," and he chose this image by Southwest artist Stephen Morath because, as he wrote to Morath, "I really like this painting." He is also attracted to Southwestern scenes.

Roland is well-known to *Celebration* readers: this is the tenth *Celebration* rug for Roland. The others were: *Hummingbirds* (XIII, 2003), *Who are You?* (XVI, 2006), *Hi There* (XVII, 2007), *Cynthia* (XIX, 2009), *Red Rock* (XX, 2010), *Bighorns* (XXI, 2011), *Lake Shore* (XXII, 2012), *Yellowstone* (XXIII, 2013), and *Yesteryear* (XXIV, 2014).

He has completed nearly 70 pieces since he began hooking as a "sit-down" hobby at 60 (more than 25 years ago),

Thornbirds, 33″ x 39″, #3-cut wool on monk's cloth. Adapted from Stephen Morath's painting Morning Moon, and hooked by Roland C. Nunn, Clayton, California, 2013. SCOTT MCCUE

yet he continues to learn from each new rug. He does not sell his pieces but shares them with family and friends.

He taught his two granddaughters to hook when they were 6 and 8. "Both now have many other interests to occupy them," but Roland hopes that they might return to this fiber art form later in life.

In the Judges' Eyes

- *Well-done interpretation of a difficult vegetative form, with great use of shading for light and perspective; enchanting use of color and texture.*

ROLAND NUNN
CLAYTON, CALIFORNIA

A familiar presence in the rug hooking community and in these pages, Roland has hooked all types of rugs: geometric, Oriental, floral, animals, landscapes, scrolls. His works have been included in guild exhibits at the Santa Clara County Fair in San Jose, California, and the Alameda County Fair in Pleasanton, California, where he has received numerous awards, including Best of Show. He also attended Pacific Grove McGown conference for 15 years.

Through the Looking Glass

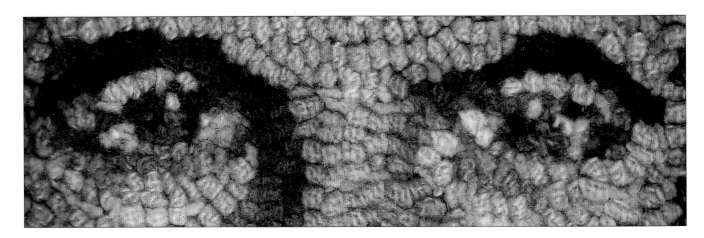

Twenty years before this 1981 photograph was taken, Kay Bowman and her husband were "a dating couple." Then they went in separate directions; each married another. Now both single again, they were being married to each other.

"The photographer had instructed us to look into the mirror, into each other's eyes. From that angle she snapped this photograph. It was our moment, hence the title: *Through The Looking Glass*. The eyes say it all. It felt natural to use my medium, wool, to record this special moment in the life of my husband and me."

Kay's dress and Keith's suit were hooked using all as-is recycled wool fabric. The suit jacket was from a man's Pendleton tweed blazer: "The colors and textures were perfect."

She relied on wool in her stash that she had simply labeled "flesh" for much of the wool used for this project. Keith's face was hooked with a purchased swatch. "By dyeing a flesh-tone swatch, and combining it with other leftover swatches, I had the wool I needed to hook my face. The hair was hooked using leftover spot-dyed wool from previous projects, as were the bells and the roses."

The bouquet was simple white roses, quite small in size, and "it was challenging to achieve the desired effect. Running out of time, after three attempts, the roses were 'shadowed,' definitely not shaded."

Kay had been been thinking about hooking this portrait for quite some time. "I started it at the 2008 Nova Scotia Rug School portrait class. I wanted to have time to give it some undivided attention, but that was hard to come by. I hooked only sporadically. During the latter years, Keith became ill. He passed away in 2012. I began to hook on it in earnest again this past summer, aiming to have it finished in time to enter *Celebration*. Six years from beginning to completion."

Through The Looking Glass is displayed on an antique easel in Kay's dining room, with its back to a sunny window. "This is a cozy room, with oak paneled walls and a mirrored sideboard. Sometimes I move it to other locations in the house."

Lessons this work taught her? "I learned that although a project can seem overwhelming, a willingness to revisit, rethink, rip out and rehook can result in gratification."

In the Judges' Eyes

- *Excellent features, with nice shading on the faces and hair, in a well-done, highly personal piece.*

KAY BOWMAN
NEW GLASGOW, NOVA SCOTIA, CANADA

Since she offered her first class, Kay has taught 177 students in an eight-week beginner's course, for which she provided patterns, dyed wool, and yarn. She is a member of the Teachers' Branch of The Rug Hooking Guild of Nova Scotia. This is her third work to appear in Celebration, *including* Anne of Green Gables (XIII) *and a portrait of her friend and mentor Sylvia MacDonald:* Sylvia (XXII).

Through the Looking Glass, 16" x 20", #3-cut wool on monk's cloth. Adapted with permission from a photo by Bonnie MacKenzie and hooked by Kay Bowman, New Glasgow, Nova Scotia, Canada, 2014.

Two Sisters and an Aunt

Kathy Peters's rug is an adaptation from a family photograph, drawn and transferred to linen by Roslyn Logsdon.

"The photo is of my mother, her sister (my Aunt Ginny, in the foreground in the brown and white suit) and between them they are holding up my Great-aunt Dorothy. It was at a family picnic at my Aunt Ginny's home on Canandaigua Lake. All three of them have now passed away. My Aunt Ginny is the only one to ever see the beginnings of this rug, and she was thrilled. She died last January at age 94."

Kathy had always wanted to take a class from Roslyn Logsdon, "and when Ingrid Hieronimus invited her as a teacher to the Niagara-on-the-Lake Ragg Tyme School of Rug Hooking in May 2013, I signed up immediately; I knew exactly which photo I wanted to do."

The class was memorable, and Kathy finished two of the ladies in the class "and finished the third when I got home. Then came the water! The photo I was working from was old and faded, but I could see that there was a wave coming from behind the people. I had no idea how to hook that, and the photo was no help because it was so faded."

She "scoured the Internet, all my rug hooking books and magazines, emailed Wanda Kerr, agonized a lot and really became totally blocked: I didn't know what do and did not hook on it for almost five months."

Finally, "I got tired of seeing it sitting on my frame and said to myself, 'Just get it done—this is ridiculous.' So I did, but it was difficult. However, I learned an enormous amount, and it taught me to really look hard and understand what is happening with motion, color, light, and reflection. I am very happy with the outcome, and a little bit proud."

Most of the wool came from Kathy's stash—some dyed by her and some by others. "I did use some of Cindi Gay's dip-dyed sky but ran out and had to improvise."

The rug now hangs in Kathy's living room over an antique desk left to her by Aunt Ginny.

"I am very happy with how the women look. They look just like themselves and just as I saw them in the lake dozens of times over the years at picnics on the beach. I am very happy also with how the water looks, especially the little wave breaking behind them."

The piece was finished with a plain and narrow antique silver frame.

In the Judges' Eyes

- *Joyful scene and great composition, effective faces done with simple lines, subtle and beautiful sky and water, lovely variety of blues; wonderful piece.*

KATHY PETERS
ROCHESTER, NEW YORK

Kathy started hooking rugs in the fall of 2001 after seeing Old MacDonald Had a Farm, *by Molly Colegrove, at a shop. "I loved it from the moment I pulled the first loop and it seemed to me that I had always been hooking." She has hooked about 30 rugs, and received two awards for* The Old Apple Tree, *designed by Joan Moshimer. It took first prize at the New York State Fair in 2009 and also earned a McGown Rug Hookrafters Guild Chapter I award that came with a $25 check. "I was just as pleased (maybe more) to get this chapter award than the first place award—it was an unexpected honor!"*

Two Sisters and an Aunt, 16⁵/₈″ x 20⁷/₈″, #3- to 5-cut new wool on linen. Designed by Roslyn Logsdon and hooked by Kathy Peters, Rochester, New York, 2014. RONALD STOCHL

UnderSea Celebration for Kris

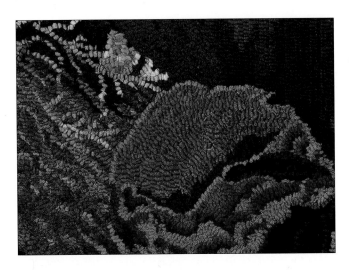

After 25 years of hooking, shading flowers remains Catherine Hickman's "favorite form of creative expression."

But when she wanted to hook a special piece for her daughter, Kris, who thought her mother should "branch out" from #3-cut flowers, Catherine asked Kris to bring a photo of something she loved.

"Needless to say, I was stunned by the complexity of the underwater photo she chose! Capri Boyle Jones's design and color plan for this rug is very similar to the actual photo by Scuba Mike. Capri added the turtle at my daughter's request." Since Scuba Mike granted only one-time use, "no one else may use or adapt this piece, so it is one of a kind."

Capri dyed all of the new and recycled wool for the project, except for the light green and white overdye used for the water. That was dyed by Catherine's first teacher and inspiration, Angela Pumphrey ("at age 95!"). The fish and much of the coral are #3-cut for detail, and the water background is #4-cut.

"Kris requested shiny embellishments but I was careful not to overshadow the underwater beauty and movement. I chose simple, shiny highlights for the fish," mimicking the effects that sunlight often creates. And "if you look closely, you can see 'fuzzy' growth in the barrel coral and on some of the plants."

In fact, Catherine's favorite part of the rug is the barrel coral in the lower center, although it was difficult to give them "craggy detail with shading" and to separate and define the plants in front using only variations of orange and pink.

The most challenging part of the rug? The turtle. "My intent was for Kris to feel it swimming right towards her. Turtles are shy creatures and are rarely photographed face-forward to the diver. I looked at countless photos and reverse-hooked a number of times to achieve this effect."

The rug was "a wonderful experience, because I am an avid snorkeler and love the colors of the sea. It was a labor of love for Kris, who is a scuba diver with advanced certification. I wanted to bring the colors and creatures of the ocean to her everyday life with this hooked piece.

"My goal was for her to feel that she was swimming into the center of the water with the sea life. Kris is absolutely thrilled with the result."

In the Judges' Eyes

- *Fabulous use of shading and color, makes the sea come to life in wool; loved the corals against the blues and the bright fish; beautiful gradation of sea-water blue.*

CATHERINE HICKMAN
SAN ANTONIO, TEXAS

Catherine began hooking with Angela Pumphrey in 1990, drawn to her "amazing" fine-cut flower and Oriental patterns by Pearl McGown and Jane McGown Flynn. Catherine's #3-cut area rugs have been shown both locally and regionally, and she is now working on a #3- and 4-cut piece by Jane Olsen. She hopes to begin the McGown certification process to learn more about wider cuts and color planning.

UnderSea Celebration for Kris, 40" x 28" unframed, 44" x 32" framed, #3- and 4-cut wool on linen, with embellishment. Adapted with permission from an underwater photograph by Scuba Mike, mauiscubamike.com. Designed by Capri Boyle Jones, and hooked by Catherine Hickman, San Antonio, Texas, 2013. SAM PIEPRZYCA, OF SAM'S STUDIO

View from the Horn

When Madonna Shelly wanted to hook a rug as a gift, based on photos of her sister-in-law's champion longhorn steer and beloved chickens, she began by collaborating with Leonard Feenan on a design.

To prepare for work on the piece at rug camp, Madonna emailed photos to her teacher, Gail Dufresne, who dyed the wool and brought it to camp. "The problem was the photos I sent to her did not show the true color of the steer; therefore, most of the wool she brought to camp did not work. We scrambled and found the correct colors in the

excess wool she had brought along." Still, "there was just something missing."

The camp store yielded a 12" x 6" spot-dyed wool "that worked wonderfully" as a transitional piece. "I used that piece to the very last strip."

The rug took about six months to complete; Madonna tries to hook for an hour or two each evening.

"The chickens were the most challenging part. In fact, a lot of viewers do not believe that they are chickens, because their combs are not standing. However, the rug is based on a

photo that was taken while the chickens were roosting; during roosting the combs do not stand.

"Hooking the feathers to look like individual feathers was the hardest. Gail had dyed some fuzzy, fun wool, and we thought that it would hook up quick and easy and look exactly like feathers. But the wool hooked up too fuzzy and did not look right with the steer. Gail had a few pieces that worked, but after returning home I dyed more wool. Ultimately, to hook the feathers to look like individual feathers, I had to resign myself to hook a loop and then a loop and cut—over and over again."

Her favorite element of the rug?

"Even though the face of the steer is quite large, I liked seeing him come alive. The nose was also quite fun, along with the horns."

Lesson learned: "Since my sister-in-law lives in Texas, as an afterthought I wanted to include bluebonnets, the state flower of Texas, in the design. No matter where I tried to place them or what hooking technique I tried, the bluebonnets just did not work. They became more of a distraction than enhancing the rug. From that, I learned not to force more into a design than what is needed."

In the Judges' Eyes

- *Fabulous background shading, unusual placement of motif, perfect shape for the image, great detail in the hide, painterly sensibility in an evocative story; wonderful composition.*

View from the Horn, 50" x 25^1/$_2$", #2- to 5-cut wool on rug warp. Adapted with permission from photos by Susan Murray, designed by The Burning Artist, Leonard Feenan, and hooked by Madonna Shelly, Granville, Ohio, 2014. BARCLAY

MADONNA SHELLY
GRANVILLE, OHIO

Madonna "cannot remember a day growing up that my mother, Marjorie, was not creating something with her hands. Even though she is not a hooker, she is the person that I would say influenced me the most for taking an interest in fiber arts." Madonna was introduced to hooking in 1997 and within a year found a nearby hooking group. "I cannot express enough how belonging to a hooking group keeps my interest and enthusiasm in hooking." She is also grateful to her husband, Mark, "for never complaining of the wool dust, noodles, scissors, or frames that are always lying around, or when I always ask his opinion on my current project."

Home From the Hunt

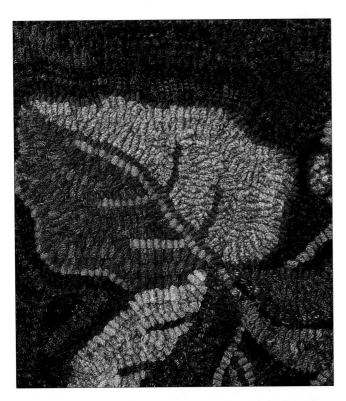

Martha Lowry did not dye any special wool for this rug that caught her eye while she was looking through a House of Price (now Honey Bee Hive Designs) catalog. Everything was already in her stash: the mostly textured wool, some as-is, some overdyed, and some thrift-store finds.

"The dog, of course," is her favorite part of the rug and also the most challenging.

"My 'teacher' for the eyes was the June/July/August 2012 *Rug Hooking* magazine, and particularly Judy Carter's article, "Eye See You." I studied this article, then did exactly what Judy recommended: I found a library book about dogs with a good close-up photo and I began to 'hook what you see.' I proceeded to follow her instructions, step by step, and the eyes came to life."

In the Judges' Words

- Great old antique quality, fantastic rendition of a beloved pet; unique interpretation of foliage and organic material, harmonious color palette; fine technique and finishing.

The techniques for the leaves she credits to "Texas teacher Susan Quicksall. The large leaves in this pattern were perfect for the technique Susan taught me for hooking leaves, so I used her method: divide the leaf in half and hook a different texture on each side. Pop the leaf from the background by outlining in contrasting wool, in a smaller cut. It was a good way to put a lot of movement and color in the background."

Hooking the shaded coat of the dog in #8-cut "could have been tricky, but I used the same principles of shading that I learned in the fine-shading classes at the McGown Teachers Workshop. I just hooked with #8 cuts instead of #3 cuts; it went much faster!"

Martha took a class from Anne Eastwood at an ATHA Biennial in braiding around a border and thought it would be the perfect finish.

"You could say I did not have a teacher for this rug—but I actually had *many* teachers. However, none of them were in the room with me at the time."

The great lesson of the rug was how to hook realistic animals in wide-cuts. And her favorite part?

Her grandson, seven, came to visit right after the rug was finished. "He said, 'Meems, this is my favorite rug you have ever made.' I added a line on the label: 'This rug is Aidan Lowry's property.' I guess this is one of my favorite things about the rug."

The rug has been exhibited at local hook-ins and the McGown Teachers Workshop.

MARTHA LOWRY
HOUSTON, TEXAS

Martha Lowry took a three-hour beginner rug hooking class at a Houston quilt shop in 2003, and in 2013 received her McGown certification. She likes to hook "everything." She hooks primitive rugs for her home, "and I especially enjoy hooking small, fine-shaded projects, because they are challenging and make me lose track of time." She hooks mostly commercial patterns but sometimes designs her own. This is her second rug to appear in Celebration.

Home from the Hunt, 28" x 42", #8-cut wool on linen. Designed by Jane McGown Flynn and hooked by Martha Lowry, Houston, Texas, 2013. JAMIE WAGNER PHOTOGRAPHY

Maine Memories

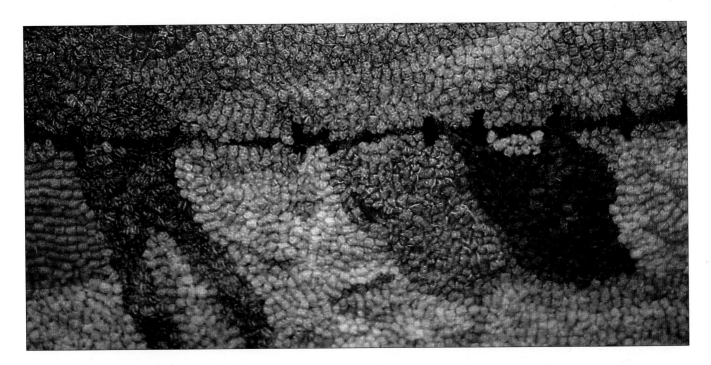

This design was a "memory rug" of Lisanne Miller's home in Maine, "hence the name *Maine Memories*."

"When I drew the rug, I incorporated all of the important aspects of my home: my yellow house on a street of all white homes, the ocean, Boon Island Lighthouse "floating" in the backdrop, and my laundry blowing in the cool New England breeze. I wanted to capture the memory of my home, not an exact duplication."

The rug was hooked with new, dyed wool. The yellow wool for the house was casserole dyed to match the color of Lisanne's house. Other wools were spot dyed and dip dyed, and the sky was "a very simple and light mottled wool."

Lisanne's favorite part of this rug is the laundry and clothesline. "By using small pieces of dyed wool and 'fussy-cutting' the dark and light values, I was able to create the laundry blowing in the breeze."

Once she began hooking, the work was completed within three weeks.

"The most challenging part of *Maine Memories* was the sky, and it was hooked last. The sky had to have movement but could not detract from the house, ocean, or the clothesline. "After trying several different dyed pieces of blue, Lisanne dyed the wool for the sky using pale gray, a hint of blue, a hint of green and yellow "to capture a true Maine sky."

The rug was finished by sewing beige wool around the piece. Lisanne finishes all of her pieces with a wool binding.

The most valuable lesson from the rug? "Stick to one color palette. I wanted almost a 'watercolor' palette for this piece and had to be sure all the colors were part of the palette." This lighter color palette was also a learning experience for Lisanne, who normally hooks in darker values.

Maine Memories was chosen as the representative piece for Lisanne and her company, P is for Primitive and Peace, Love & Wool, by *Martha Stewart Living* as a "Made in America" craft/company.

"Each of us is gifted in many different ways. Rug hooking allows me to explore and expand the world of fiber arts as well as my artistic abilities using design, texture, color and balance. Creating new pieces of art that hold secrets of a previous life makes every rug an adventure."

In the Judges' Eyes

- *Lovely color palette, sweet subject matter, simple and well-balanced composition; very sweet, heartwarming impact; loved the yellow-gray blue combination and the motion of the billowing clothing.*

*Maine Memories, 16" x 18", #3- to 5-cut hand-dyed, spot-dyed, and abrashed wool on rug warp.
Designed and hooked by Lisanne Miller, Canton, Mississippi, 2013.*

LISANNE MILLER
CANTON, MISSISSIPPI

*Lisanne Miller is a self-taught artist who first hooked a chair pad at age 14, which was stored away
until, years later, a friend shared her interest in rug hooking. Since then, Lisanne has "never looked
back and never put her hook down." She was recently named a Fellow Master Craftsman of the
Craftsmen's Guild of Mississippi and a Top-40 Artist. She is an ATHA board member, president
of The Magnolia Wool Dust Society, ATHA Chapter #114, a magazine and book contributor,
and teaches privately and at schools and workshops across the country.*

OSVP–155, Totem Pole

Nancy Campbell purchased this rug from a friend at a local hook-in sale. "I thought it would be fun to hook with bright colors. Plus, a friend of mine loves Alaska, and I planned it as a gift for her."

Nancy prefers to work on linen, but the piece is on burlap. "I was going to transfer it but would have had to darken the lines, and I felt that doing another transfer of the pattern would alter it—so much small detail. So I hooked on burlap for the first time."

The wool in this piece is all new, some as-is, and some overdye purchased from Donna Hrkman.

Nancy began the rug at a summer 2013 rug camp with Donna, and finished it in August 2014. "This was my rug to carry to meetings. I rarely worked on it at home. The size made it easy to transport."

She loves the richness of the colors and the brightness of the blues, reds, and greens. "Lately, many of my primitive rugs have been subdued." She also liked the fact that each motif was unique, with no repetitions.

"Color is always a challenge: it's what makes a rug. First I looked at several books and online sources for pictures of totem poles, choosing what I liked best in colors. I had two copies of the rug pattern made to size. These I colored in with pencils. Donna said it was best to start with this: spread colors throughout the pattern, create continuity (example: eyes all the same color). Also, I would not work myself into a corner if I had a color plan." She used the first day of class choosing colors of wool, then coloring the paper pattern.

"Then I was ready for hooking itself! I must admit to a few color changes—not many. But having color-charted made the project easy to do."

Although she prefers a wool border on her rugs, "I felt this needed something very simple. I folded the linen and simply whipped it with 100 percent wool to match the background."

Lessons learned: "Coloring a pattern first is a nice way to get a picture of what you are doing. It is easier to experiment with than hooking and taking it out," especially with so many non-repeating motifs.

"Until I saw rug hooking I was a busy cross-stitcher. Now—I'm a hooker. Love it! The wool! The people! The friendships! The giving and sharing!"

This rug was exhibited at Sauder Village in 2014.

NANCY CAMPBELL
KETTERING, OHIO

"I first noticed a very small and expensive mat in Ohio's Amish Country. I loved the look and thought: 'I can do that!'" She found a class in 2000 "and my rug hooking began." She has hooked about 30 pieces, ranging from coasters to rugs, always in primitive style. She uses commercial patterns on linen, but "tweaks" them with personal preferences and family references. She is a member of Miami Valley ATHA Guild #98. This is her first rug to appear in Celebration.

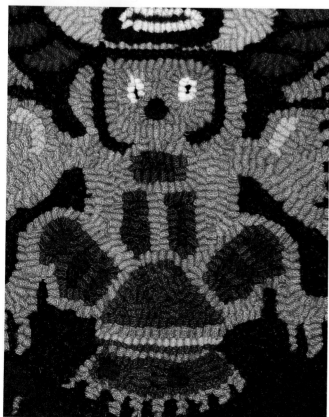

OSVP-155, Totem Pole, 8¹/₂" x 33", #4-, 6-, and 8-cut wool on burlap. Designed by Pearl McGown and hooked by Nancy Campbell, Kettering, Ohio, 2014. KERRY BERKEY

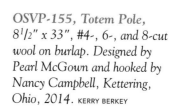

Star Flowers

"I chose this pattern several years ago because I loved the playful qualities of the design, with its padulas (imaginary flowers), stars, and wonderful leaf border. Over time, the number of objects in the design began to seem too busy, so when I finally did get it out to hook I eliminated a lot of extra berries, twigs, and flowers."

Jan Winter used a small amount of dip-dye and spot-dye, but most of the wool, new and recycled, is overdyed textures and solids as well as off-the-bolt wool.

"My favorite part of the rug is the central star flower. I love how the bold, darker rays form a base support for the center of the flower. The colors of the circles in the center have a nice rhythm that keeps your eye moving. The attached flowers have a little highlight that keeps them from looking too flat."

She started the rug with a much darker turquoise background and yellow and orange stars. "It wasn't working at all because the colors were too extreme. I pulled all of that work out." The final version took about two months to finish.

"I had to rethink my background. It needed to be lighter, but with some dull qualities to it, so that the brighter flowers would stand out without being too garish and one-dimensional. I had planned on making the edge around the leaves a darker purple, but the leaves got lost in it. Then I had to darken the leaves to seem like a border. I didn't think I had enough of the center color to fill in the entire background, so I had to dye and introduce some other versions of blue tweeds to fill it out. I was barely left with one 4" strip when I finished!"

The rug is finished with a whipped yarn edge through twill tape, which is then stitched flat, with mitered corners.

"I think I re-learn the same thing from each rug that I do. That is: Whatever you think about how you will proceed, at some point the rug tells you where you are going wrong and where you need to adapt your ideas. Colors that look like they have enough value difference while sitting loose on top of the background fabric can look darker or duller when their textures are compressed into loops. You can never have too many values of the same color for depth and variety. Always remember to add darker, duller, lighter, and brighter fabrics for contrast."

JAN WINTER
HOLLYWOOD, CALIFORNIA

Jan Winter is the founder of the Cambria Springs Rug Camp, now directed by Gene Shepherd. She studied and worked with Jane Olson for 19 years. Jan has created many original rug patterns, some of them appearing as Celebration finalists by other rug hookers. "Since I lacked an aptitude for drawing, I think that fabric, with all its wonderful colors and textures, provided me with a way to be creative that I hadn't foreseen. The sewing machine gave way to hand sewing and led to rug hooking." This is her eleventh piece to appear in Celebration.

Star Flowers, 25" x 48", #6- to 8-cut wool on monk's cloth.
Designed by Woolley Fox Design and hooked by Jan Winter, Hollywood, California, 2014. JOE WOLCOTT

Vintage Blooms

"Mom taught me early in life to appreciate antiques so I have a love for anything old, used, and worn."

After discovering a floral pattern in a book of antique rugs, Theresa Rapstine Schafer thought "how fun it would be to try and replicate." She made some sketches and her husband, Rich, helped her square it off and adjust it to size.

Theresa had signed up to take Cindi Gay's workshop that summer "so we worked via email on the pattern and colors. I was thinking it should look like the original—to honor it. However, Cindi encouraged me to think about a border, one that would start at the edge of the rug and move inward by four inches."

Theresa arrived at class with recycled wool, overdyed plaids, and solids "in a very large suitcase. I wanted to 'use up' the camel-colored recycled wool I had collected, so I started with this as the background color. After several hours of color planning, Cindi said to me, 'Hook like you don't care—and just keep going.'"

Theresa occasionally looked at the original picture, "but soon the colors spoke to me and began to take over each flower."

After finishing about a third of the rug, she put it aside. "I wasn't sure if it was right, and I didn't have the confidence to keep going."

The following year, she took the rug back to camp, where she showed it to Cindi, Barb Carroll, and Cynthia Norwood. "Each gave me great feedback. My teacher that year was Sharon Smith; she asked me what I thought about adding more of the blueish green color that I had in the leaves. I'm not a big 'blue' fan and this was my biggest challenge. But, I thought I would try it (I always listen to my teacher), so I went home and added the blue flower (thank you, Sharon Smith)."

After a year or so, "what you see now is a 'group rug'—made with input and feedback from many teachers, my husband, my Denver ATHA group, my cross-stitching friends, and my Mom. Each comment shaped the next color, the flower, the background and the border. My favorite part of this rug is its story—its many artists—and how it was inspired by the past. This rug proudly lays in our living room in front of the French doors."

In the Judges' Eyes

- *Primitive through and through; hooking like brushwork, loops with textural quality; soft color palette with the strong contrasting border for impact; "imperfect" aspect of elements create overall primitive feel; really love the border on this rug.*

Vintage Blooms, 36" x 72",
mainly #10-cut with some #8.5-cut
as-is, hand-dyed, and recycled wool
on linen. Original design inspired
by circa 1900 rug (property of The
Society for the Preservation of
New England Antiquities at the
Beauport-Sleeper McCann House
in Gloucester, Massachusetts).
Hooked by Theresa Rapstine
Schafer, Denver, Colorado, 2013.
COLLEEN HENNESSY

THERESA
RAPSTINE
SCHAFER
DENVER, COLORADO

Theresa bought her first rug
hooking kit at an outdoor antique
festival. She pursued it off and
on, encouraged by her mother,
who loved it, but it wasn't until
about four years later, when she
took a class with Karen Kahle,
that she fell in love with rug
hooking. "I didn't want to leave
her class." Theresa is a pediatric
nurse, completing a Master's
degree in nursing. She is ponder-
ing her next floral, in teals,
inspired by a painting by her
grandmother. This is the first
appearance of her work in
Celebration. *This rug appears*
in the book Primitive Hooked
Rugs for the 21st Century, *by*
Cynthia Norwood, Stackpole
Books: May 2015.

*1830 Eagle, 46" x 56", #6- and 8-cut hand-dyed wool on linen.
Designed by Karl Kraft and hooked by Joan H. Strausbaugh, Biglerville, Pennsylvania, 2014.* A.J. ARBOGAST

*A Dozen Roses,
37" x 24", #4- to 6-cut
custom-dyed, off-the-bolt,
and overdyed repurposed
wool on linen. Designed by
Fritz Mitnick and hooked
by Kathy T. Stephens,
Bozeman, Montana, 2013.*

Child of the Universe, 30" x 30", #3-cut wool on linen. Designed and hooked by Grace Collette, Chester, New Hampshire, 2014.

Mont St-Michel, 46" x 31", #3-cut wool on rug warp. Designed and hooked by Fumiyo Hachisuka, Tokyo, Japan, 2013.

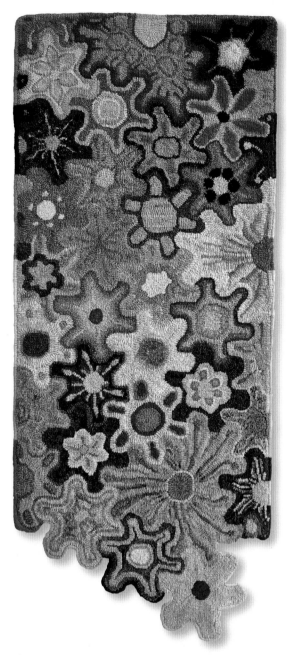

Dance at Bougival, 19^1/$_2$″ x 39^1/$_2$″, #3- to 6-cut wool on rug warp. Adapted from a painting by Pierre-August Renoir and hooked by Karen Whidden, Southern Pines, North Carolina, 2014. JOHN WHIDDEN

Moods, 14″ x 32½″, #4-cut wool on rug warp. Designed and hooked by Lil Quanz, Baden, Ontario, Canada, 2014. KEN QUANZ

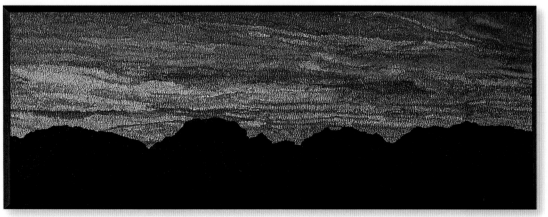

Sundance Peak, 16^3/$_4$″ x 39^3/$_4$″, #2- to 4-cut wool and lamb's locks on linen. Designed and hooked by Diane Ayles, Huntsville, Ontario, Canada, 2013. TYLER AYLES

*Mallard Ducks, 16" x 16",
#2- and 4-cut wool on linen.
Designed by Jon Ciemiewicz
and hooked by Val Flannigan,
Kelowna, British Columbia,
Canada, 2014.* GRAEME FLANNIGAN

*Henry and Veda Meinert,
21" x 16", #5-, 6-, and 8-
cut wool on linen. Designed
by Laura Pierce from a family
photo and hooked by Paula
A. Meinert, Christopher,
Illinois, 2014.* PAUL HEIDBREDER

Leaf Tango, 44¹/₂" x 30", # 6- and 7-cut wool, and Lopi, wool, and rayon chenille yarn on linen. Designed and hooked by Patty Rosencrantz, Oriental, North Carolina, 2014.

Lizzie, 84" x 64", wool and silk yarns on linen. Designed and hooked by Gail Dufresne, Lambertville, New Jersey, 2013.

CINDY MACMILLAN

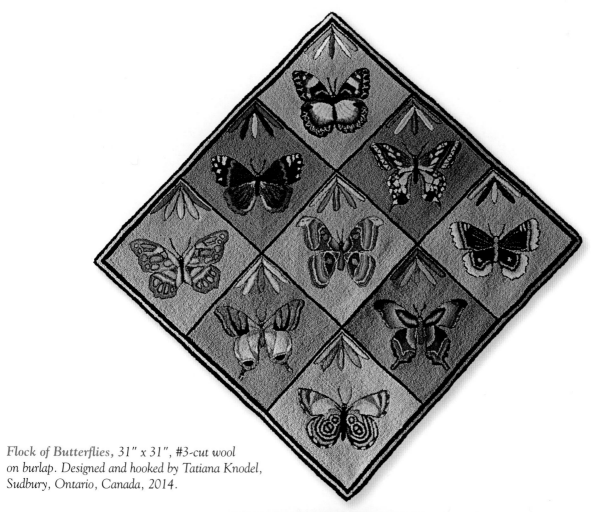

Flock of Butterflies, 31″ x 31″, #3-cut wool on burlap. Designed and hooked by Tatiana Knodel, Sudbury, Ontario, Canada, 2014.

Mailman Carter Wedding Rug, 37″ x 25″, #6-cut as-is and dyed wool and wool threads on rug warp. Designed by Leonard Feenan and hooked by Judy Carter, Willow Street, Pennsylvania, 2014.

Milking Time, 31¹/₂" x 23¹/₂", #5- and 6-cut wool and denim on linen.
Designed and hooked by Kitty Speranza, Skamokawa, Washington, 2014. DAN FAZIO

Ella in Camo, 15" x 17", #3-cut
wool on linen. Designed by Donna
Hrkman and hooked by Judith Kehrle,
Toledo, Ohio, 2014. JOSH MILLER

*The Western Island Georgian Bay, 36″ x 18″, various cuts wool on linen.
Designed and hooked by Kathryn Taylor, Toronto, Ontario, Canada, 2013.*

*Mrs. Rabbit, 24″ x 35″,
#4- to 7-cut as-is and dyed wool
on linen. Designed by Sharon
Smith and hooked by Cheryl M.
Bell, Mexico, Missouri, 2013.*

CHRISTINA UNGER

Shadow Hills, 18″ x 12″, #2- to 4-cut hand-dyed wool on linen.
Designed and hooked by Myra Bielby, Edmonton, Alberta, Canada, 2014. YUET CHAN

Slater, 18¹/₂″ x 24″,
#5- and 6-cut wool on
linen. Designed and hooked
by Patricia Helland, Gig
Harbor, Washington, 2014.

OWEN CAREY PHOTOGRAPHY

*Mountain Aspen, 37" x 26", #3- and 5-cut wool on linen.
Designed and hooked by Charlene Kerber, Clovis, California, 2014.* STEPHANIE WATERS

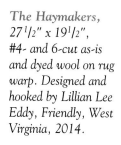

*The Haymakers,
27¹/₂" x 19¹/₂",
#4- and 6-cut as-is
and dyed wool on rug
warp. Designed and
hooked by Lillian Lee
Eddy, Friendly, West
Virginia, 2014.*

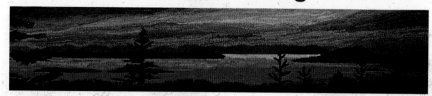

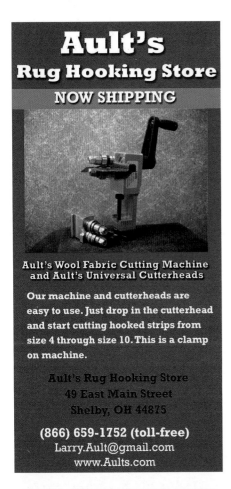

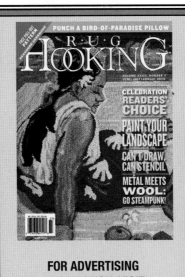